Manly Piety in its Realizations

Manly Piety in its Realizations

Robert Philip

Waymark Books

Copyright © 2023 by Waymark Books

This is a proofread and newly designed edition of a public domain work.

CONTENTS

1. On Manly Realizations of God in Hearing — 1
2. Manly Realizations of God in Devotion — 15
3. On Manly Realization of God in the World — 32
4. On Manly Realizations of Final Judgment — 43
5. Manly Realizations of Invisible Things — 58
6. Of Manly Realizations of Glory in the Church — 71
7. On Manly Realizations of Christ in the Bible — 89
8. Manly Realizations of Future Probabilities — 102

1

On Manly Realizations of God in Hearing

The preaching of the gospel is "the ministry of reconciliation;" and God so identifies both His character and authority with it, that it is, "as though God did beseech us to be reconciled" unto Himself. The apostles believed this, and preached the gospel of the kingdom as the ambassadors of the King; urging reconciliation on the world, and on the church, in the very spirit in which God and the Lamb would press it, were They to preach their own gospel, or plead Their own claims in person. This was taking very high and holy ground, indeed, as ministers of the gospel! We concede to them, however, the right of placing their preaching on such vantage ground. They were well qualified to sustain and justify their title, when they stood forward in the face of the world, saying, "We are ambassadors for Christ." They could demonstrate the legitimacy of both their office and their embassy by miracles, whenever it was necessary to prove them by such signs or wonders; or, they could rise to such heights of wisdom and eloquence as accorded with both the loveliest and the loftiest views of the God in Whose name they spoke. Their reasonings were not unlike His manifold wisdom; nor their appeals unlike His paternal kindness; nor their remonstrance unlike His judicial authority. Thus there was much that was godlike in their preaching. We readily feel and confess this. We see at once the "demonstration of the Spirit," in the boldness of Peter, in the sublimity of Paul, and in the heavenliness of John. When we think of them as preachers, we feel quite sure that we should have recognized and revered them as the messengers of God. We can even revel in imagining the delight with which we should have hung on their lips and sat at their feet.

But, when we try to transfer this feeling to uninspired preaching, how its fine spirit changes. Both its love and liveliness evaporate the moment we attempt to transfer them from apostles to modern evangelists, in general. Towards a few modern names, we can, indeed, easily transfer no small portion of that veneration and deference we feel for the apostles of the Lamb. Transcendent genius, learning, or eloquence, commands homage somewhat akin to what we pay to inspiration; but towards men of like talents with ourselves, we are slow of heart to attach any importance, beyond what their superior piety wins for them. Is this altogether creditable to us? It is, indeed, very natural: but is it wise? True, it would be unwise to identify ordinary ministers with inspired apostles. It would be impossible to do so, even if it were not improper. It is, however, highly improper. No man, however gifted or holy, has any right to such deference as we give to the first ambassadors of Christ: and to give it to every good man who preaches the gospel could only lower our respect for inspiration itself. Besides, no really gifted or good minister would thank us for identifying him with the apostles. But, after all, it was the truth the apostles preached that was the main thing, even in their ministry. Neither their gifts nor their graces added an iota to the goodness of the good tidings they proclaimed. Their miraculous powers gave no saving power to the gospel. Miracles accredited its truth, and demonstrated its importance; inasmuch as they were all too good to be the vouchers of a lie, and too great to be the seals of a trifle; but they added no glory to the glorious gospel itself; they only illustrated and attested its inherent glory. They proved the greatness of the great salvation; but they did not, could not, make it any greater in grace or glory than it was before the world began.

That salvation is therefore no less, now that miracles and apostles too are gone. It lost nothing of its grace or its glory when it lost their services. The covenant of grace was "well ordered in all things, and sure," before they ministered at its Ark; and it was nowise deranged or altered when they were withdrawn. The gospel is still, and as much as ever, the ministry of reconciliation now that ordinary men proclaim it, as when its ambassadors were like mighty angels flying in the midst of heaven to preach it. We forget what reconciliation with God is, if we doubt or do not feel this. That message of mercy would be majestic beyond all comparison and comprehension, even if babes were the messengers, or the birds of the air its bearers. "Be ye reconciled unto God," is a voice that should arrest and charm us at once, and equally whether hymned by an angel, or hummed by an insect. No human tones can render this good news harsh, and no human nor angelic talents could render it more worthy of our acceptance. We forget our alienation from God, or underrate the peril of it, if there be not celestial music to our ears and hearts, in any and every whisper of reconciliation.

I am no apologist for harsh tones or inelegant terms in preaching the gospel; but I must say that if either can turn us against the gospel, or even lower it at all in our estimation, we do not love it as we ought, nor feel our need of it much. It cannot be lessened in the esteem of any man who believes it cordially, by the manner of any man who preaches feebly or coarsely. Well-regulated minds will, indeed, feel grieved, just in proportion as they are warm-hearted, when the glorious gospel is tamely preached; and disgusted, when it is disgraced by vulgarity or levity. These feelings will, however, terminate upon the man who excites them, and in nowise extend to the truth he utters. It will be revered by believers, however much he may be pitied or despised.

It is of great importance to cultivate such an adoring sense of "the word of reconciliation," that no form of stating, or delivering it, can weaken our love to it; and this is not impossible. We have only to ask ourselves, whilst hearing a very poor sermon on the subject of salvation, 'Would I not be thankful even for this faint glimpse of the cross, if I could obtain no other? Would it not bind me, beyond all release from the obligation, to lay hold on Christ for eternal life? It is, indeed, a poor exhibition of a rich subject; but still the Savior is in it—the call of God is in it—the promise of the Spirit is in it; and all so in it, that I could not excuse myself to Father, Son, or Spirit, if I were to neglect Their great salvation, although thus feebly set before me. I dare not say, at their tribunal, that the poorness of the sermon prevented me from embracing the richness of their grace. Thus any sermon which indicates, however dimly, the way of acceptance with God, and which whispers, however weakly, the welcome to believe and be saved, is such a message from God, as renders unbelief or indifference utterly inexcusable.'

This is not, however, the general character of evangelical preaching. Its average, if plain, is not common-place, more tame. Were it, however, both, it would still be the best source of wisdom and consolation that our world furnishes. I have no objection to join any one in deploring poverty of thought, feeling, or language, wherever it is found; and none to condemn that poverty, wherever it is the effect of idleness; but after all the deductions and objections which can be made, I must hoodwink both my judgment and conscience before I can cease to see that the most ordinary preaching of the gospel is infinitely better than all that is extraordinary in the appeals of nature, or the discoveries of philosophy. Of evangelical preaching, as of Christ, it may be said, "To whom else can we go? Thou alone hast the words of eternal life." The words of poetry may be found in nature, and the words of patriotism in philosophy, and the words of wealth in science, and the words of amusement in literature; but "words whereby we can be saved" as sinners, or soothed as sufferers, or cheered at death, are found habitually and systematically on no human lips but the preacher's. His lips keep the knowledge that makes wise unto salvation.

I know and love the voice of nature, from its softest whispers up to its loudest thunders; from its tinkling rills up to its roaring cataracts. I have listened to her voice, both in her Edens and her wildernesses; on her mountain-thrones and in her ocean-caves; on the bosom of her seas and in the depths of her forests; under both her sunlight and moonlight; and asked all manner of questions in these scenes: but all in vain, whenever the questions touched upon immortality or salvation. Then nature was as silent as the grave; her light was darkness, and her loveliness proved nothing, until I opened my Bible. Men may talk of finding:

"Books in running brooks,
Sermons in trees, and good in
Everything;"

whilst the only good they seek or feel the need of is temporal. Sermons from trees and flowers, rocks and stars, may answer their purpose whilst the soul cares for nothing but its own capacity of interpreting and enjoying the aspects of the creation; but when the soul feels that its powers are responsibilities, and that its eternal prospects are clouded by guilt and depravity, no sermons but such as Peter preached at Pentecost can relieve its anxieties. Accordingly, men soon quit the temple of nature when they begin to ask, "What shall I do to be saved?" Only the house of God is a temple then; and then it is a temple, even if its minister is an itinerant. Let him only be a good man, and mighty in the scriptures, and his weakness in any other ministerial qualification will not be thought of by a soul thirsting for salvation. As the feet of the messengers of peace were "beautiful on the mountains," although disfigured and torn in running from the camp to the city, to make the good news early news to the fearful, so the humblest preacher of the gospel, if his heart be in his work, will be loved "for the truth's sake that dwelleth in him," by any man who feels the need of that truth. He will not, however intellectual or refined, refuse to be comforted until "a master in Israel" preach to him. He will gladly take the cup of salvation from the first hand that offers it full; and, although he may soon seek some stronger hand to fill it again, he will never forget, or cease to bless, the hand that filled it first. In like manner, if he is a lover of nature, his return to her temple, although sure, will never be at the expense of the

| 5 |

sanctuary of God. He will wander and muse again in his favorite walks, but not at the time of the Sabbath morning, or evening sacrifice. He will still love solitude and scenery, but he will not prefer them to the ordinances or the fellowship of the church.

It is not, however, necessary, in order to maintain the importance of preaching, to rest the argument upon the case of those who are crying out or longing for the water of life. Men, who will not, of course, are very fastidious in their taste. The claims of preaching can, however, be justified apart from all appeals to the timid or the trembling. Even that kind of preaching, which never won applause by its eloquence, nor kindled public curiosity by its fame, has made Britain and America whatever they are as "holy nations," and much of what they are as free and powerful nations. Most readily and cheerfully do I grant, yea, contend, that the great preachers of both nations gave the impulse which rendered preaching popular, and made ordinary preachers enterprising. They won or compelled much of the homage which the pulpit enjoys in both hemispheres. Without these high priests there would have been fewer Levites, and the Levites less successful. The tall cedars of Lebanon have sheltered its fir, olive, and myrtle trees, when the tempest has broken on the mountain of the Lord's house. In this point of view, great men have done great good by their preaching. It has "greatly helped" ordinary men to be useful. But still, it has not been by wonderful sermons, but by wise and warm-hearted sermons, that most good has been done. The great majority, both of the dead in Christ and of the living in Jerusalem, were won to Christ not by the giants of genius or erudition, but by the watchfulness and fidelity of hard-working pastors. The claims of the pulpit do not, therefore, rest upon the memory of its brightest ornaments. They rest far more upon its countless converts. Its "record is on high." The general assembly of just men made perfect will be its great cloud of witnesses. All who will have washed their robes in the blood of the Lamb will be the vouchers and the trophies of its instrumental triumphs. The pulpit—the ordinary pulpit has always been the chief means of filling heaven. The eloquence of the senate has occasionally freed nations from despotism; and the eloquence of the bar, from conspiracies against liberty; and the chairs of science and philosophy have often dissolved popular superstitions; and all these triumphs have wrought together for good to the souls, as well as to the bodies of men; but the conversion of souls to God, and the training of souls to glory, have been the achievement of the pulpit. No other "chair of verity" can point forward to the multitudes that will surround the eternal throne, and say, "Behold the children whom God hath given me." The pulpit will say with truth of all the redeemed from amongst men, "All these souls are mine," instrumentally; whereas it is more than doubtful whether there will be one soul in heaven, to whom any thing on earth was so useful as preaching. Neither literature nor legislation, science nor philosophy, can trace their triumphs in that world. They are all "of the earth, earthy;" for whatever influence they have had upon any one in heaven, the gospel made it heavenly.

In thus magnifying the pulpit, I do not forget the mighty influence of good books and godly parents in directing souls to heaven. I claim, however, the best of both for the pulpit. All the most useful religious books emanated from it, and almost all godly parents were its children. It trained the fathers and the mothers who have trained up their children in the nurture and admonition of the Lord. Whatever we owe directly to pious parents, we owe indirectly to the pulpit. It has, therefore, no occasion to throw its defense or its claims upon the sun-stars which have shown in it from time: the ordinary stars of its holy galaxy have been the chief lights of the world, in leading many sons to glory; and its brightest stars themselves were kindled by it.

But whilst the grand record of the pulpit is "on high," it has also a goodly record below. The history of preaching, like all other history, is, indeed, disfigured, and even stained, by crime and folly. Nothing too severe could be said against the nonsense and noise, the quirks and cant, the servility and extravagance, which have often issued from the pulpit. Still, on the other hand, nothing too kind or too grateful can be said of the moral and ameliorating influence which, notwithstanding all these faults, it has had upon the character and condition of this nation. In nations where preaching is a secondary thing in public worship, public worship has but little moral influence. It does not tell well upon law or order. It neither purifies social life, nor improves public opinion. Itself a form, it gives nothing but form to morals and demeanor; whereas, wherever the pulpit is as sacred as the altar, both tell powerfully upon public and private life. We are more affected, and perhaps not improperly, by what the pulpit fails to accomplish, than by its beneficial influence on the community. The good it does makes no parade of itself; whereas the evil it cannot reach, or fails to cure, obtrudes itself upon our notice in rampart forms. Any one can tell what the pulpit has not done for the nation; but, it is not every one can calculate what it has done, or comprehend the amount even when it is summed up. I frankly confess that I cannot. I have often tried, but always failed: never, however, without determining to try again. Failure always inflamed curiosity. I can easily and at any time see what God has done by the pulpit, whilst I number its living converts and its dead vouchers; whilst I look at the order, and listen to the domestic worship of all the families in the land, whom it has taught to fear God; whilst I pass from congregation to congregation, and church to church, marking how many in each it unites in heart, and how many of the united it confederates in the glorious work of teaching, visiting the afflicted, and spreading the gospel. I can even see, with some clearness, how the preaching at home creates and keeps up all the agencies, which are now shaking idolatry and superstition abroad.

But, whilst I can thus trace the influence of the pulpit as its "line is going out through all the earth, and its words to the end of the world," I cannot trace that line as it runs through all the frame of society, strengthening good laws, and pushing out bad forever; giving integrity to trade, and honesty to policy; working out the freedom of slaves, and the equal rights of freemen; turning national patriotism into universal philanthropy; making the arts chaste, the sciences modest, and literature moral. Here I am lost I know that the sanctifying and sustaining line blends itself with all that is good and great, in national character and public spirit, and moderates all that is bad or base in both; but it is so widely extended, and ramifies itself so minutely, and works so calmly, that, like the principle of gravitation, it eludes the eye, although universally felt. As in the sea, although all the rivers run into it, they so soon blend themselves with its own waters, that the stream of the mightiest river cannot be traced far upon the bosom of the great deep; but still they all uphold its volume: so, in society, the distinct influence of preaching is felt through all its frame, but is indefinable as affects the whole frame. Perhaps, therefore, the best way of estimating its beneficial influences is to ask ourselves, 'What would be the consequence of extinguishing the pulpit?' Suppose it extinct and forgotten; and thus all the families of the land thrown upon their own mental and moral resources, guideless, creedless, and without Sabbaths or sanctuaries; how long would British liberty be the day-star of the world; or British philanthropy be the hope of the heathen, or the home of the destitute? How long would property or life retain their present sacredness: Let France answer these questions. She tried to do without either the pulpit or the altar of God; but, although science, policy, and heroism put forth all their energies, in union, to make her the queen amongst the nations, they made her only the beacon of the world, and the victim of her own impiety and caprice. I am, therefore, not ashamed to "magnify my office." It is God's ordinance, and gloriously has he owned and honored it in the world.

What, but preaching, overthrew ancient heathenism all over the Roman empire? What, but preaching, broke the iron scepter of modern Rome? What, but preaching, by the agents and energies it has called forth at home, has added the islands of the Pacific to Christendom, and brought the idolatry of India to a crisis which fills even its priesthood with despair? Most fully and frankly do I concede, that the pulpit is neither what it ought to be, nor what it might be: but still, I fearlessly maintain that, even as it is, nothing else does so much good, nor could any thing be invented in its room that would do more or equal good. Any mode or system of teaching that was less elementary would be useless to the poor; and one more elementary would be unedifying to the intelligent and the educated. Whatever, therefore, a few fastidious minds may think or say, who take more interest in the poetry and the philosophy of religion than in the conversion of sinners, or the consolation of saints, it can be proved, indeed it requires no proof, that their ideal pulpit would answer no practical purposes. They themselves are living proofs of this. Their refinements, whether sublimated thought, or exalted feeling, terminate upon themselves and never lead them out to teach the ignorant, or soothe the wretched. The utmost that these sentimental critics of the pulpit do is to sentimentalize a few of the young, who happen to have little sense and less care. And they must have very little of both to listen to idle men pitying or despising working ministers. It is well for the world that ministers have not such refinements as such critics plume themselves upon. If they had, they would soon be as useless as their critics.

Look always, therefore, at the whole state of the world, before you fix a standard to judge preaching by. The pulpit ought, indeed, to keep pace with the march of intellect and the progress of knowledge. It should never be in the rear of the school, nor its ministers behind schoolmasters. The march of intellect, however, does not outrun the march of suffering and sorrow; the progress of knowledge does not stop the progress of death or disease. The hereditary ills of life follow society like its shadow, however society advance. The pulpit must, therefore, adapt itself to the permanent mass of suffering, as well as to the accumulating mass of knowledge. There must be no such haste to overtake intellect as would hurry a minister away from softening calamity. Breaking hearts, and bleeding consciences, must not be sacrificed nor forgotten in order to keep up with expanding minds or exploring spirits. He is, therefore, as "cruel as the grave," although polished as a cenotaph, who prefers the gratification of his own literary taste to the comfort of the tried and tempted, the disconsolate and bereaved. The mental food he calls for would be mockery to the wants and woes of suffering humanity, and moral poison to the souls of the thoughtless. And yet, there are men so selfish and mean, as to writhe with impatience, or to manifest disgust, when preaching weeps with them that weep, or woos them that tremble, or guides them that mistake. This is pitiable, yes, contemptible, in the extreme! A well-regulated mind, however original or powerful, would rejoice to see preaching condescend to men of low estate, and especially to mourners in Zion. That mind is both ill regulated and ill disposed, that grudges milk to babes, or balm to wounded spirits. It may dream of seraphic ardors and angelic ideas, but there is not a seraph, nor an angel in heaven, has any sympathy with the vulgar and vitiated taste of that man who revolts at experimental sermons, or frowns on efforts to cheer the weary and heavy-laden. Fallen angels only sympathize with his taste.

I cannot conceive a better test of a well-balanced mind than a disposition to take a lively interest in whatever is likely to be most useful to the greatest number, and to the chief varieties in a congregation. There is comprehensiveness as well as candor, strength as well as tenderness, in the mind that follows the "dividing of the word of truth," when the minister is giving to every one "his portion in due season." It thus goes round the circle of the various wants of real life and godliness, and by linking its sympathies with them all, proves that it can recognize in each want and woe of other minds what may become its own case at a future time. And the good sense and good feeling thus evinced, are both invigorated by the habit of marking how the gospel furnishes "a word in season," to all the varieties of human experience. Such a hearer is not tame nor tasteless, because he is not impatient for his own portion whilst greater sufferers are receiving theirs; nor because he continues to look and listen with interest after he has received his own: for, whether waiting patiently for it, or watching afterwards the distribution of the bread of life to others, he is laying in a stock of experimental knowledge which will save him from many mistakes, and come to his help when his soul may be in darkness or distress. Nothing, therefore, is more false than the notion that no good can be got from a sermon which is not personally interesting to us. If it be really suitable to any one, it may be useful to us, because the case it meets may some time be our own case; or, what is better, it may prevent us from involving ourselves in the dilemmas of such a case. Paul evinced as much philosophy as philanthropy when he said, "Look not every man on his own things, but every man on the things of others also." He did not mean by this that we should "hear for others," but that we should learn from what suits them, as well as from what is adapted to ourselves. Besides, it is, although not in the popular sense of the word, truly, "fellowship" with the Godhead, to take a lively interest in the spiritual welfare of all classes under the gospel.

The man who has been reconciled through the blood of the cross participates in the paternal feelings of the Father, and in the mediatorial solicitude of the Son, and in the gracious sympathies of the Holy Spirit, when he forgets his own personal joy, in the joy of hearing others beseeched to be reconciled unto God. The man who has but few cares, and no perplexities, never has more fellow-feeling with the Eternal Mind than when he melts with pity, as the successive trials and temptations of penitents and pilgrims are exhibited and met. We come, also, into sublime fellowship with "the innumerable company of angels, and with the general assembly" of heaven, when we listen with delight to sermons calculated to lead sinners to repentance, and adapted to teach penitents to bring forth fruit meet for repentance. In all this our spirits would delight, were they in heaven, looking down from the throne to the pulpit; and, surely, it is not less becoming, when looking up from the pulpit to the throne.

You are now somewhat prepared for the unqualified assertion, (for, as I could not qualify it, I delayed it until now), that the kind of preaching which some call for is not provided for in the word of God, nor agreeable to the will of God, nor suited to the real wants of the world: I mean, the demand made by minds of a certain order for flashes of imagination and feats of reasoning. This class cares for nothing but talent and taste in the pulpit. Now, if there were nothing but talent and taste around the pulpit, I would be among the first to maintain that more ought to be put forth in it. Reasonings might be more profound and illustrations more splendid without at all darkening doctrinal or sentimentalizing experimental truth; for, whilst there is nothing so lowly as the gospel, there is nothing so lofty. It demands simplicity, but it admits of sublimity. Is that really sublime, however, which a few literary men, and not a few youthful minds, regard as such? They recognize no sublimity in sermons which set the spirit to commune with itself; nor in sermons which lead the spirit into communion with the Father; nor in sermons which place all souls in the only position in which a sinner can find mercy. Are they, therefore, competent judges of the sublime or the beautiful in thought or feeling, who have thus no relish for the grand ends of either? What real glory can there be in any line or form of thought which does not lead the spirit in upon itself in scrutiny, and out to God in supplication? That only is grand in idea or diction, which brings God and man into willing communion with each other. The splendor of all thought which carries away the heart from Him, or draws it to Him in any other character than as the God of salvation, may resemble the genius of devils; but it has no affinity to angelic eloquence, and is no prelude of those "Thoughts that breathe and words that burn," in heaven. The only truly sublime ideas are those which will be eternal ideas, when the mind is all light, and the spirit perfect.

Consider this: evangelical preaching brings before your minds, from Sabbath to Sabbath, all the grand truths which you will admire and love to all eternity in heaven. If, therefore, you think and act with any express reference to the eternal themes of heaven, and the emotions of your spirit, you cannot but rejoice that the pulpit gives prominence to the truths which the throne will prolong forever. The notes which preaching gives of the new song may be weak and unequal, but they are all key-notes of the everlasting anthem of redemption. And this, you know, cannot be said, with any semblance of truth, of the kind or forms of sentiment, which mere literary taste, or mingled taste and fancy, regard as most sublime. That is most sublime which sublimates taste, to relish what is the chief joy of immortals, and what Deity forever approves.

I may now, surely, call upon you to admire both the wisdom and kindness of God in committing the ministry of reconciliation to the trust of ordinary men. "We have this treasure in earthen vessels, that the excellency of the power may be of God, and not of man;" and in earthen vessels of various dimensions and polish, because the treasure is intended to enrich minds of all orders, and men of all conditions.

2

Manly Realizations of God in Devotion

Whatever propriety there may be in bowing our knees and lifting our hands before God when we worship Him, it would certainly be impossible to love or fear God if either postures or sounds amounted to acceptable worship. It might, indeed, from our natural aversion to thoughtful and spiritual devotion, please our slothfulness, and suit what we call our convenience, if a humble position of the body or a solemn vocal sound would pass for worship: but, if they did, we could not think highly of God. He would not rise in our estimation by thus lowering His demands to mere "bodily service." For, however unwilling we may feel to "worship Him in spirit and in truth," we are absolutely incapable of admiring or adoring a God who could reckon Himself worshipped without "spirit and truth." Accordingly, He is neither loved nor revered by those who content themselves with forms of bodily service. His character and authority stand just as low in their estimation, as the level they bring his services to. They see nothing attractive or trustworthy in God and the Lamb. They are merely afraid or ashamed to neglect all the forms of religion.

These facts deserve more notice than they usually receive. We are very ready to suspect, when we hear much about the necessity of spiritual worship, that it would require more time and involve more attention than is compatible with a due regard to the ordinary business of life. We even try to make out a case against it, as impracticable or impossible. We allow, indeed, that something ought to be, and may be done, in the worship of God; but we very much doubt whether a uniform habit of spiritual devotion could be combined with temporal enterprise and enjoyment. It seems to require more leisure than the busy command, and more thought and feeling than the active can afford. Thus we exaggerate and caricature its claims, by making them to clash with the duties of life. This is unmanly; for it is not true that spiritual devotion makes any demand upon our time or attention beyond what we can pay without temporal loss or risk. No man can prove that an honest business would be injured by a devotional spirit. Business and prayer have been divorced by the vast majority of tradesmen, but the trade of the country is no real gainer from the separation. There is more of it, but it is less healthy in its action, and less sure in its results, than when it was more religious in its character. Our pious forefathers seldom failed to realize a competency by their business. Their credit was not shaken nor their ultimate success hindered by their regular habits of closet, family, and public worship. They made less noise and dash in conducting their business, but they "guided their affairs with discretion to the end." The balance-sheet of no single year enabled them to vie with the mansions or the equipages of hereditary wealth, but the balance-sheet of successive years enabled many of them to retire from public life in sober affluence, and kept most of them in easy circumstances. If they had no sudden elevations, they had no sudden downfalls; and in old age, what pictures of vigorous health, and venerable gentility, our pious ancestors were! The rose was upon their cheek, and "their gray hairs were a crown of glory" over it. They equally won and commanded respect by their perfect urbanity, and decorous manners. All eyes either blessed them in the gate, or blushed in their presence. Neither the fops nor the nabobs of business, however successful, obtain any such hearth-homage now, from the young or the old. The reason is obvious; they are men of the world; altogether of "the earth, earthy." Nothing about them beams or breathes of immortality. By no effort or stratagem can the opening or the enlarged mind link their lot with grace or glory. It is opulent or showy—that is all. And is that enough to live for? No, not even if all the appearance, and the reality too, were as easily obtained as they are naturally desired. But that, they are not. Besides, what is a man profited, if he gain the whole world, and lose his own soul?

Men of business are, in general, calculating men; but no class of men, who have credit for this prudential faculty, are more chargeable with "reckoning without their host." In general they do not take God into their account at all, except to postpone His claims to the last. They adapt none of their measures for getting on in the world to the maxims of His grace or providence. His great moral laws against fraud and circumvention are, indeed, both recognized and revered in all honorable business, to a very great extent. They must be so: business could not go on without them. But how few merchants or tradesmen have the wisdom to pause at the outset, or in their progress, and ask themselves, "What will be best for me in the end? I may get on in the world without religion—many do. But still, I may not; for many do not. Even clever men are not always fortunate men. Should I, however, be fortunate in this world, there is another world; and in it, I cannot be happy. I must be forever miserable without religion. I, indeed, both hear and think about becoming religious in the evening of life, but I must confess that I see very few who do so. I join with others in hoping the best in the case of those who die decently, after having lived only for this world; but I feel that I should not like their chance for my own soul! I do not venture to pronounce or conjecture on their state; but neither durst I venture my soul upon their soul's probabilities. I cannot wish to die their death! It may be safe, but it is too suspicious to hazard my soul's wellbeing upon." How few of our calculating men calculate even in this way; and yet, this is little more than the plain application of plain common sense, and common honesty, to the consideration of familiar facts.

Indeed, it would only be good common sense to grapple fairly with the question, "What must be the natural effect upon my own mind, of leaving no adequate time for prayer? I have many temptations to dispense with it now, and for years to come. I am getting so placed and pledged in the world, that I want all my time for my business. An immediate attention to closet piety seems utterly incompatible with my immediate interests. It would be more convenient for me to lay aside all devotional piety, until I am more settled in life and business. Is it, however, quite sure, or at all likely, that I would become prayerful, when I had got on somewhat well in the world? Now years of neglect are certainly not likely to produce a mew era of inclination to prayer. Might they not rather extinguish all sense of its necessity, or disincline me more than I mow am: Besides, it cannot be safe to calculate that God would answer prayer years hence, even if I could calculate upon myself for becoming prayerful then. For, why do I wish to keep clear of the closet now? It really is because I care more about this world than about the next: more for time than for eternity: more for human things, than for the divine favor? This is the fact, if I must speak out; and it is all naked and open to God, however I may conceal it from others. Now, is not this enough to prevent Him from answering prayer, even if I did pray much and fervently, after having served myself at the expense of His immediate claims? In a word, would I bear such treatment from any man, as I have thus thought of giving to God? Were any man dependent on me for all his support and comfort in the evening of his life, to plan how much he could avoid me, until he could no longer do without me, would I welcome him when sheer necessity alone forced him to apply to me? True, God is not like man in this matter. Many have come to Him late, and yet have found both mercy and grace. But, they did not plan to come late, nor delay in the face of such convictions as I feel. My neglect of prayer for the sake of business would be deliberate neglect. I see clearly both the sin and the shame of the liberties I am tempted to take with God. The real question, therefore, in my case is, not how God may treat the late prayers of those who do not know what they are about, but would He answer my late prayers? I do know what I am about, when planning to keep clear of my closet. I cannot plead ignorance of

MANLY PIETY IN ITS REALIZATIONS

either the duty or the danger. Shall I, then, dare to "sin willfully?" Ah, my convenient "season" could not be "an acceptable time." Even my own conscience tells me so."

These, also, are not very profound calculations; but, simple and sober as they are, they are not very common. They are, indeed, glanced at, when they glare upon the prayer-less; but how few invite them, or go fully into them, even when they force themselves upon the consciences? And it is not painful calculations only, that are avoided: prudential reckoning is not common. A special Providence is acknowledged in words, but denied, indeed, almost defied, in practice. How else could any man dream that the way to do well in the world is to put religion quite aside for years; is, to push on without prayer; is, to banish all concern about the soul and eternity? No man can show that this is a likely way to keep Providence on his side for good. It is, indeed, often a successful way, but always for evil of some kind.

Success is a very ominous thing when it is obtained apart from piety. No misfortune nor poverty is a token of so much danger to the soul, as prayer-less prosperity. The "evil things" of Lazarus were certainly trying things: but the "good things" of Dives were curses in disguise. I do not mean, of course, that there is nothing but judgment in prayer-less prosperity. There may be much mercy in it, for a time. God may allow it, in order to give the man every facility for becoming a pious man. For as some natures are so stubborn as to require the rod to bend them; others are so weak, or so mean, as to require some temporal blessings to conciliate them. They would not think of God at all, if nothing went well with them. In pity, therefore, to such minds, He places them in circumstances which furnish no excuse for the neglect of His great salvation. When, however, prosperity itself is perverted into an excuse for neglect and delay, then the blessing begins to 'rot into a curse. Dives' purple and plenty are then omens of eternal ruin; and will end in that, unless they are taken as warnings of it.

Would I then have a man to care nothing about success in business? Certainly not. A man utterly indifferent about his lot in this life is not likely to care much for the life to come. Success is a good thing, when obtained by good means, and applied to good purposes. Success is also a sure thing in our world now, because the church is thrown upon it for the means of evangelizing the world. Christians, acting as Christians, are as sure to get on, as the cause of God is to go on. Business need be no lottery, now that the gospel is spreading. Providence will take care of their interests, who are devoted to His glory. Both the silver and the gold are His, and he will make them run in the channels where the best use will be made of them. They will not flow long upon the old channels. They ran into the hands of the ungodly, whilst there was nothing but conquest and commerce to push over the earth; because such hands were fit for nothing else. But, now that the world is thrown open to the spiritual conquests of the church, wealth will change hands, because "the Lord hath need of it," for his own work. I do not mean, of course, that all his poor will become rich, nor that the existing rich men of the world will be impoverished; but, I do mean, that Providence will gradually "turn the tables" upon trade, and give the market of the world to the men who do most for the salvation of the world.

God will not starve nations hungering for the bread of life to pamper individuals who loathe it, or grudge the expense of spreading it. Their old times are going as fast as the kingdom of God is coming. Neither Boards of Trade, nor Chambers of Commerce, can long sway the world against Boards of Missions and Bibles. Every regenerated nation, although it will not reject ungodly traders, will give the preference to godly traders; and consign to Christians what capitalists have hitherto monopolized. Worldly men will not believe this, I know; and Christians will be afraid to believe it. It is, nevertheless, true. Just as true as that the gospel must be preached unto all nations; which it can only be, by transferring, in the course of Providence, the means of sending it into hands that will send it. The time is, however, hardly yet come for unfolding this mystery to the church. She is not prepared yet to do business for God, on God's principles: for she has not studied them much. She has something like a settled conviction that no man is "a loser by what he gives to the cause of God;" but the philosophy of this proverb she does not understand. And the church will be unable to understand it by study. The proverb, like prophecy, will only explain itself by its fulfillment. Its truth will not come out by searching for it; but evolve gradually, as good men, from disinterested motives, adjust their business to the principles and spirit of the gospel.

What I want to teach now, therefore, is the criminal folly of running in the face of Providence by trying to get on in the world without God, or without such a regard to His claims as amounts to devotion. Now, although this may not hinder success, it will, and must, render success a curse and not a blessing in the end. It may gain the world, but it will ruin the soul. It will not, however, save the soul, to combine devotion with business, for the sake of gain. That process would end as fatally as the plan of separating them ends. Providence can neither be bought nor bribed over to any man's side by selfish prayers. It may come over to his side, and is likely to do so, when he is more concerned about eternity than time; about his soul than his circumstances; but it will not strike a bargain with him, to pay for prayer in money or bills. The grand object of prayer must be the salvation of the soul. Other blessings must neither be expected nor sought for, but as they are conducive to that end, and to the promotion of the divine glory. It is not necessary, however, to keep the temporal bearings of Providence out of sight, lest they should tempt us to selfishness. God has brought them into sight, and therefore they should not be overlooked nor underrated. "Godliness is profitable unto all things, having the promise of the life that now is, and of that which is to come." Thus God asks no one to serve him for naught, nor sends any one on a warfare at his own charges. What is good the Lord will give, and what is evil He makes to work for eventual good, unto all that love him.

It is, therefore, both a willful and gross mistake to suspect that we should be losers by devotional piety. Many of the pious are, indeed, very poor; but they would be still poorer than they are if they were not pious. The design of all these preliminary hints is, to solicit and conciliate your attention to that "fervency of spirit, in serving the Lord," which the Lord connects with "diligence in business." Now "God is a Spirit, and they that worship Him must worship Him in spirit and in truth." Such only are "true worshippers;" and, as the Father seeketh such to worship Him, thus we should seek to pray. Mark the words! "The Father seeketh such to worship Him." He finds them, unsought in heaven—and, shall He seek without finding, on earth? Will you refuse to "worship him in spirit and in truth?" In the spirit of love and truth, He invites and beseeches you to draw nigh to His mercy-seat, believing that He "is the rewarder of them that diligently seek Him." Can you refuse to seek, when God thus assures you that you shall find all things really "pertaining to life and godliness?" Remember, God will permit none to draw nigh to the throne of glory who refuse to draw nigh to the throne of grace. All who keep afar off from the latter will be kept by "an impassable gulf," far off from the former. Pray or perish is the only alternative. Can you wonder at this? Is it a hard or a harsh alternative? Consider! You must allow that something should be done to prepare for heaven. Now could you name anything easier than prayer which would be equally adapted to prepare your spirit "to meet God" in peace and glory? Try. You cannot. Nothing you can think of would have the same tendency to pave the way for the worship of eternity. Oh, the wonder is, that prayer is permitted! And that the Father should seek us to worship Him, is wonder unspeakable.

"The Father seeketh" spiritual worship! Again, I ask, shall He seek in vain from you? You will need such a Father through all eternity. You may soon need all His paternal pity in time: for you know not what trials may await you on earth. Should trials be, however, both few and slight in your lot, still you need such a Father to be its guardian and glory. There is no moral loveliness, no dawn of heaven, in the splendor of godless prosperity. Its garlanded votary is a doomed victim to the judicial altar of vengeance. And the Judge will find you, if the Father seek you in vain. "The Father seeketh you!" Oh, let this sublime and solemn fact seize upon all the powers of your soul, and sink into all the recesses of your heart. He seeketh not fallen angels. Yes, with less effort than He puts forth in seeking you, even by a word or a wish, the Father of your spirit could create myriads of spirits, all of whom would vie forever with the first created spirits in the universe in worshipping Him. But He loves better to redeem human spirits than to multiply angelic spirits. He prefers to seek and save a lost sheep to creating new orders of worshipping intelligences. He wants the old order on earth brought nigh to him, before He begins another creation in heaven. He seeketh you now. He will not, however, seek you always as a Father, nor for worship. He may soon seek you as a Judge, for punishment: and then He will find you out. You may evade His call to the throne of grace, but you cannot evade His summons to the bar of judgment. You may refuse to pray, but you cannot resist punishment. Why, then, should you risk it, seeing the Father seeketh you to worship him?

When Martha said to Mary, "The Master is come, and calleth for thee," Mary, "as soon as she heard that, arose quickly, and came unto Jesus." Now you approve of her promptitude: you would have blamed her if she had not gone at once, when He called her. Why? If, because it would have been unwise, ungrateful, unsafe, and thus exceedingly sinful, to neglect or evade the Savior's call whilst He spoke on earth; then, remember, and apply to yourself Paul's solemn oracle—"See that ye refuse not Him that speaketh; for, if they escaped not, who refused him that spake on earth, much more shall not we escape, if we turn away from Him that speaketh from heaven." When Paul weighed this awful consideration, he immediately applied it to himself and the believing Hebrew thus: "Let us have grace, whereby we may serve God acceptably with reverence and godly fear: for our God is a consuming fire." This is a long appeal; perhaps you are tired of it. Do you, then, really so dislike prayer, that warnings against the neglect of it irritate and vex you? Can you defy them recklessly, or defeat them by stratagem? Do mark well the precise state of your own feelings at this moment! If the law of prayer "work wrath" in you, and if your heart can rise and writhe against it, are you not yet "in the gall of bitterness, and in the bond of iniquity?" How can there be "any good thing in you, towards the God of your Fathers," if you hate to draw nigh unto Him in that spirit which He requireth from all who worship Him? This reluctance must be looked into. It is not the feeling of the moment, chased only by remonstrance; it is your natural spirit breaking out in its inherent and hereditary aversion to "worship God in the beauty of holiness." And this spirit will not go away of itself. It will grow upon you if you do not grapple with it at once, and at all hazards. The force of direct effort, however, will not subdue it. No, nor will the power of solemn warnings put it down. There must be consideration as well as excitement; hopes as well as fears, before our natural reluctance to spiritual devotion can be overcome: for the Spirit of grace and supplication works by both; and therefore we ought to employ both.

Now, one consideration which I have found to be very useful is this:—"Were God as reluctant to answer prayer, as I am to pray with the understanding and the heart, how alarmed I should be for my soul! And yet, why should He care more for me than I care myself? If I grudge the time, thought, and feeling, requisite to plead my own cause seriously, why should God take any interest in it, or the Savior take it up in His intercession? God and the Lamb will not, cannot—nor can I expect them to do so, whilst I myself do not think my own salvation worth asking for." Thus, by asking ourselves how we should like God and the Mediator to feel and act towards us, in the matter of answering prayer, we see at a glance how They must require us to feel and act toward Them in praying for mercy and grace. Do not then mock God by neglect or formality, if you would not provoke God to "mock when your fear cometh." You know it will come. The time is coming when you will be glad to "pour out your heart before Him" with strong cries and tears. You intend to do so. You would do so now, if you were sure that you would never have another opportunity. Yes, if you strongly suspected that you may be unable or unwilling to pray on your death-bed, you would make a decided stand now against your reluctance, rather than risk the awful peradventure of a seared conscience or a delirious understanding at last; for you cannot bear the horrid thought of dying insensible or insane, hardened or helpless.

Another consideration which I have found to be very useful is, "How small, in itself, is the point on which I am standing out against God? I am not unwilling to be moral in my life, nor to be sound in my creed, nor to be regular in public worship, nor to do some good, according to my power, to the poor and the perishing. I can go on with some heart in public work and worship; but I stop, I stand out, at my closet! There, both my good principles and feelings break down shamefully. And at what? If it were at the idea of spending hours every day in my closet, there might be some excuse for shrinking back now and then from secret prayer. But I know better than to imagine that "long prayers" are required or expected. I may talk to others or to myself about the want of time, and the pressure of business; about care in the morning, and fatigue at night; but I cannot hide from myself the fact that I find time for things of far less importance than prayer. I contrive, notwithstanding all the pressure of labor and fatigue, to read a good deal, to amuse myself not a little, and to improve myself somewhat in my favorite tastes. True, I require this relaxation. Both body and mind need to unbend after being on the strain all day. Health and spirits would break down altogether, if the routine of daily labor were not cheered by some exhilarating pursuit. All this is true; but what does it prove? Why, this, that I could find time for prayer too, if I had as much taste for it as for the pursuits in which I relax myself. Besides, if health or spirits be dear to me, I am really periling both by heartless prayer; for, however music or painting, literature or science, may soothe the mind after care and fatigue, they cannot insure health or spirits. I am entirely dependent upon God for both. I cannot place myself out of the reach of His "mighty hand" by any stratagem. Am I not, therefore, provoking that hand to strike me, whilst I am all but prayer-less? Thus, even upon my own principles, that something is necessary to diversify and lighten labor, lest health break down under it, I am imprudent, as well as criminal, in holding back from "fervent prayer."

"Ah, it is not the time it requires that holds me back. I am unwilling to give my heart up to the objects and emotions which belong to prayer. This is the real fact, whatever I may pretend. I am not indifferent about my soul or salvation; but I have no such love to them, as loves devotion for their sake."

Have you not? Then you love something more and better than the salvation of your soul; more and better than you love eternal life. What is that something? Whatever it be, you cannot get it, nor keep it, in spite of Providence, however much you love it. Indeed, if it be not a sinful object that your heart is set upon, you are taking the sure way to miss or lose it, by thus preferring it to the great salvation. God will not bear with this preference. He will either cross you in it, or curse you with a portion in this life. And if the object of your preference be sinful, you are arousing all the perfections of His character against your soul. Do look at the awful dilemma you thus place yourself in! It is very awful, however laudable in itself may be the object you now love more than salvation: for you cannot get it and salvation too, whilst you prefer it to salvation. God will never place his gift of eternal life in the left hand of any man who gives his right hand to an earthly portion. God will not lay His great salvation beneath the feet of your little projects. He will have it and make it uppermost in your heart, or He will give you up to your heart's lusts. You cannot escape Him. Down your idols must come, or down your soul must go. This is the only alternative. Providence will either cross you at every step, until you are heartsick of the world, and glad to give all your heart to salvation; or curse you with success until you are conscience-seared with prosperity. This is the invariable rule of Providence. It mends or ends the mam to a certainty, by some means. You are doing God great injustice, and your own understanding no credit, if you think this a harsh process, or a hard alternative. It beams and burns with love throughout. It is all tender mercy in its intention. God could not do you a greater kindness than set His providence against the things which you prefer to His salvation: for, if He should not do so and thus leave you to take up with an earthly portion, you would deplore it in the end; whereas, in all eternity you would adore Him, should He even lead you "through fire and water," to the wealthy place of glory.

It is not however, necessary to bring matters to this issue. Neither your soul nor your circumstances need be thus periled. The alternative set before you now, is not the loss of all the world, or the loss of your soul. It is this—will you give your heart to your eternal interests from choice, or compel God either to break your heart with adversity, or to harden it with prosperity? Thus the choice you are called on to make now is not between salvation and adversity. What is really "good" for you in this life, God will give you, from the very moment you "seek first the kingdom of God and his righteousness." He knows all the other things you have need of, and he will add them to the gift of eternal life, whenever you lay hold upon it, in a spirit becoming its value and holiness. This, then, is the real connection in which God seeketh you to worship Him in spirit and in truth. He seeks you to do so for the sake of your own interests in both worlds, as well as for the sake of His own glory. Can you, then, refuse any longer to pour out your heart before God in secret?

Are you now resolved to "enter into your closet, and shut the door, and pray unto the Father, who seeth in secret, and rewardeth openly?" If so, enter, wondering and adoring that you are permitted to appear before God alone. You would not like friends, nor strangers, to hear the matter or the manner of your first fervent prayers. You have that to confess and deplore, which they ought not to hear. God does not want them to witness your "strong cries nor tears." He wants all your secrets for Himself, and He will tell none of them to any one. He will inform angels of your repentance, that they may rejoice over you; but He will draw no human attention to what passes between you and Himself, except as He drew that of Ananias to Paul, by simply and delicately saying, "Behold, he prayeth!" God did not tell Ananias all that Paul told him in secret. In like manner, He will not betray your confidence when you confess your sins. He will humble you by revealing Himself to you; but

He will not mortify you by exposing your case to others. Closet secrets are sacred with Him. David knew this, and prayed thus: "Put Thou my tears into Thy bottle." Enter your closet, also, determined to be thoroughly honest before God. Do not attempt to hush up any thing, however painful it may be to confess freely. "If your heart condemn you, God is greater than your heart, and knoweth all things" already. You cannot impose upon Him. All things in your heart and your history are naked and open to the eyes of the God with Whom you have to do.

> "He knows the words we mean to speak,
> Ere from our opening lips they break."

Do not, therefore, try to conceal or equivocate on any point. The point to which you feel most reluctant, because most ashamed to come, is the very point to begin at, in penitential confession. If you fail or falter there, your general confessions will all go for nothing. They will not even pave your way to the point which you thus dread and dislike to come to. Come to it, therefore, first and fully. You can easily go into general confessions of sin and shortcoming. They are sure to follow, if the great matter between God and conscience is honestly and humbly gone into.

You know what I mean. Every "heart knoweth its own bitterness," and what embittered it, too. Now, be that what it may, what it is, in your case, you must go fully into, and fully through with. To palliate it is to mock God, and to hurry it over is to trifle with Him. The very inclination to evade it and shrink from it shows that you either love the sin still, or that you would fain throw the blame of it upon anything rather than on yourself. This will not do! The single fact, that you have turned it over in your mind so much and so long, in order to divide the blame between yourself and others, is itself proof that you are deeply to blame. Conscience would not bring it up so often, nor fear shrink from it so instinctively and constantly, if you were not the chief criminal. There was, of course, temptation, and there may have been strong temptation, and even some deception practiced upon you, but you were not duped without your own consent. Accordingly, you would not deem yourself innocent, or only half to blame, were you to yield again to the same force of temptation. True, you now know the consequences of yielding, and thus are more upon your guard; but you then knew that God had forbidden the sin, and yet, in the face of his interdict, you tampered with temptation, until you fell before it. Thus, you defied Him then at all hazards; a crime which you can never palliate, whatever wisdom you may have learned from experience since. It is not without occasion that I thus enforce thorough humiliation before God. You know that your heart holds back here. You are inclined to skirt the edges, or to skim the surface of your own case, and thus to hush up what most needs to be gone fully into. And nothing needs such a full disclosure before God as the sins and the idols which have hitherto made you ashamed, or afraid, or unwilling, to be alone with God in your closet.

You will not, however, be thoroughly honest or humble in your closet, even now, if you go there to meet God, only as a God who will not be trifled with, and cannot be deceived. You never will like to be alone with Him for confession, until you are as much alive to His love as a Father, as to His omniscience as God. You must realize His eyes as beaming to pardon iniquity, if you would not shrink from them as burning "to mark iniquity." Their paternal mildness—their looks of love, pity, and solicitude, form the only lasting link between the heart and the closet. You will not come to God there often, nor continue long, until you firmly believe that "He is the rewarder of them that diligently seek Him." Prayer, almost hopeless, will soon become altogether heartless. Only believing prayer will be persevering prayer. Remember, therefore, that it is as a Father, God seeketh you to worship Him. He is a Spirit; but He is a paternal Spirit. This should touch your heart to its inmost core, for you know what this means. Either from the experience of paternal tenderness, or from the want of it, you can judge of the worth and warmth of the love of God. "As a father pitieth his children, so the Lord pitieth them that fear Him." And if this cheering fact do not open on you in light and loveliness, emanating from home-associations, you can at once supply their place by the memory of the prodigal's father. He was what God is. God will welcome you, as he did his lost son. Let this sink into and settle in your heart, whenever you retire to pray. This is not the reception you deserve, after keeping away so long from your heavenly Father. He might justly upbraid you, and that bitterly too; but He will not. He will leave all his reproofs to your own self-upbraiding. He will trust the fidelity of your conscience to the melting of your heart as you listen to Him, saying, "This my son, was lost, and is found; he was dead, and is alive again." He will leave His love to produce its own effect, by folding you in His arms, until you feel the beatings of His own heart pressing on the throbbing of your heart. Be not staggered at this strong language. Remember again, that God seeketh you. The father of the prodigal ran to him, when he saw him afar off; but he did not go in search of him to the city of his extravagance, or to the fields of his wretchedness. We know of no step he took on his behalf until he saw his face turned homeward. He saved the lost then, but he did not seek him before. God has, however, often sought you, whilst you have been wandering, and shunning him. You have often felt that He was seeking you to return. Sometimes the drawings of His Spirit were so strong in your spirit, that you knew not how to resist them. You have felt Him bring you to a stand, and leave you utterly without the shadow of an excuse for wandering a moment longer. You feel something of this now.

Oh, let all these considerations prove to you that God will welcome you in the closet. He would not thus seek you if He were unwilling to receive you. Do then seek Him, Who thus seeketh you that He may save you. I wrote in a figure, because I wrote feelingly, when I said that God would fold you to his bosom as the prodigal's father fell upon his neck and kissed him; but you know what I mean. God's promises of pardon and acceptance amount to as much as if He did all this literally. What He says and swears in His word is as true as if you saw him lift His right hand to the heavens, and heard Him swear to you by His life, that He has no pleasure in your death. Now, you would go anywhere to see and hear this. Enter, then, into your closet, open your Bible, and realize all that God is, from what it says of Him and for Him; and what less do you find at the mercy-seat than an embracing Father? What more could He show by voice or vision, than that He is as much and as essentially love as He is a Spirit. Now, if all this does not reconcile and win you to secret prayer, what probability is there that you ever will be won? You may well tremble for yourself, if you are yet disposed to keep away from your closet. Take care God may shut you out, if you do not shut yourself in, this night. He is now within, calling for you to enter, and commune with Him; but once the Master of the secret house of prayer is "risen up," and ye begin to knock, He will say unto you, "Depart; I never knew you."

What shall I say more to commend or enforce devotional habits? Do you yet feel averse to them? If by any ingenuity you can still evade them, you are far gone in "the snare of the devil." Where, then, may he not lead you, if he can already keep you away from that closet—where God awaits to be gracious; where the Savior manifests himself to the soul; where the Holy Spirit helps infirmities, and sanctifies the heart; and where all find by prayer the grace which leads to glory? Arise, for the Master calleth thee! The Father seeketh thee to worship Him. Say to him, with David, "When thou saidst, Seek ye my face; my heart said, Thy face, Lord, will I seek."

3

On Manly Realization of God in the World

Were there a spot on earth or in the universe, which God could not see, or where God would not look, it would be no desirable residence, however starred with natural beauty, or rich in all that could gratify the senses. It would only be but just better than hell, whatever were its scenery, society, pursuits, or pleasures. There is, however, no such spot in all the infinitude of space. "The eyes of the Lord are everywhere, beholding the evil and the good." Were there, however, a place, here or hereafter, where we could be as much invisible to God, as God is invisible to us, would we prefer it to an abode where "all things are naked and open unto God?" This question, although fanciful, and even founded on fiction, is not useless. It will bring to light both facts and secrets of the heart, which we do well to consider. Suppose, them, that there were a place on earth, where God took no account nor notice of what was done or felt by its inhabitants; where no religion was expected, and no punishment followed sin; would it have any attractions for us? Would we, in order to escape accountability and observation, prefer it to our present responsible place, if it were in all other respects comfortable? I am not supposing a place of torment, solitude, or desolation; but one exactly like the bright and busy scene we are now in, in all things but religion. Let all the arts and sciences be in it; all the forms of trade and commerce; all the ordinary charms and charities of social life, and the whole mass of human literature, luxury, and amusement. Look at it now steadfastly, and observe how you feel— whilst you think of business that Providence would never cross; of pleasure, which had no perils; of weeks which had no Sabbaths; of nights and mornings which required neither prayer nor praise; of death, which had no terrors; of an eternity, that would be quite as good, in all respects, as time. How would such a world suit your taste? Would it be pleasing, were it possible? Would you prefer this freedom from all religious duty and spiritual danger, to being as you now are marked and remembered at every step by God, and bound over to appear at the judgment-seat of Christ?

Many, you are aware, act as if our world was just such a world as I have supposed. My fancy-picture is only their real-life history, so far as their wishes go. They wish for all these exemptions from present duty and future danger, and even try how little they can think about either. Would you accept a real exemption from both, if you could get it? Would it gratify you to have nothing to do or fear, through time and eternity so far as God is concerned? Now, however you may feel in the grasp of these questions, it is quite certain that many would be very glad to be thus released from all religious obligation and future accountability. You know many who would be quite in their element, in such a world as I have imagined. They would be more than contented; they would be delighted with such liberty. Let us then look at them, observing minutely, and jealously, how far we are inclined to choose or wish as they do. This process, also, will bring to light the secrets of the heart. These are not easily got at in their real forms. We are very ready to give ourselves credit for yielding rather to the force of circumstances than to our own inclinations, when we neglect or compromise in religion. We often ascribe to the want of ability, or of convenience, negligence which ought to be traced to a want of good-will towards duty and devotion. Most of our "cannots" are really, "will nots," however reluctant we may be to confess the fact to God or man. The extent, however, to which this is true, is not very easily discovered. Hence the necessity of plying ourselves with all kinds of questions, which place our hearts before ourselves, somewhat as they are seen by the heart-searching God.

Take, them, a man who would be glad to have nothing to do with God. Suppose him exempted from all duty and danger, here and hereafter; what has he gained? Anything you envy? True; freedom from all fear is a great thing. This you never have had. This you may never obtain on earth. Would you, then, prefer the absence of all fear to the presence of some good hope, through grace, of being loved by God now, and eventually elevated to live with Him forever? Could you dispense with a hope full of immortality, if you might have a lot void of all care, and a heart void of all fear? Would you exchange the prospects of eternal life in the divine presence, and of entire conformity to the divine image, for the possession of a world without God? If you would, or at all feel that you could do so, it is high time for you to take the alarm at your own tastes and inclinations. They are "of the earth, earthy;" yes, there is much that is both sensual and devilish, as well as brutish, in them. What? Content to be forever like man as he now is, when you may be forever like God, in the purity of His character, and in the perfection of his happiness? Content to be forever what you are, when you may be forever all that angels are in bliss and beauty? Content to bear forever the image of the earthy, when you may acquire "the image of the heavenly," in all its splendor of intellect and glory? No, no; surely not. This would be to forego "angels' food," for husks. You were made for better things; you are capable of higher pursuits. Eternity cannot exhaust the life nor the energies of your spirit. Infidelity alone can bound your knowledge or you happiness. Seraphs have no joys which you may not reach, and archangels no glory which you may not realize. You may be, in body, all that the glorious body of Christ is; and in soul, all that the eternal Spirit of Holiness can make you. And then the material universe would be the range of your studies; the intelligent universe the circle of your friends; the Godhead the source and center of your bliss; and immortality the duration of all this "exceeding weight of glory." Can you still fall back upon an earthly portion? Do your thoughts or feelings fall from this heaven of heavens, to seek a more kindred element in a world without God?

Do mark your own emotions and tendencies, whilst your spirit is thus "caught up into the third heavens." You see the bent of your mind now. Your heart is naked and open to yourself. You feel that you are less in love with heavenly things than you suspected. You gave yourself credit for more goodwill towards future glory than you now find to exist within your spirit. Thus, the image of the earthy is broader and deeper upon your soul than you imagined. Oh, it is not without infinite reason that the Scriptures say, "Ye must be born again." The necessity of a new heart and a right spirit is no "marvel," when we look at either the enjoyments or the engagements of heaven. You see, at this moment, that our natural taste for them is any thing but strong or habitual. Part of what you feel at present, however, is, no doubt, partly owing to the kind of view we have just taken of heaven. It is too intellectual and abstract to reach the core of the heart, or even touch its most sensitive points. I do not mean, of course, that the view is at all beyond your comprehension. You have often, no doubt, soared higher and circled wider in your realizations of eternity. I mean therefore, by "intellectual and abstract," in this view of heaven, that it has appealed to you rather as intelligent than as accountable; rather as rational than guilty; rather as judging creatures than as sinners passing to the bar of God to be judged. Now, this is not a fair view of heaven; and, therefore, the heart has not fair play when it is tried by a merely intellectual test. God does not try it in this way. He sets heaven before us as sinners who deserve hell; as sufferers who need rest; as mortals who love immortality; and this I have not done here. It is, therefore, partly my fault that you have felt less interested about heaven than you wish to do. There is, however, only too much truth in some of the glimpses you have got of your own heart, whilst I questioned and cross-questioned its tastes and tendencies. It is not from instinct, nor from natural choice, that any one prefers conformity or accountability to God. If left entirely to our own bias, a holy heaven would have no attractions for us. We could content ourselves in a world without God, if it were not worse than this world. It is, therefore a mercy that we have no choice but between heaven and hell; and no alternative but to submit to the government of God here, or to see our end hereafter; for were we not thus "shut up" to choose between eternal life and the second death, even heaven, in any of its revealed glories, would have but few moral charms for our earthly minds.

But it may be said, "What has all this to do with the omniscience of God?" I answer, at once, "Much every way;" for it is not every recognition of His heart-searching eye, that can keep the heart from taking up with an earthly portion, or bring the heart to choose a heavenly portion. It is one thing to admit as a matter of course, that God sees us; and quite another to be so penetrated with the conviction as to pause often beneath His eye, saying, with solemn awe, "Thou God, seest me." Any one, even a deist, will confess His omniscience; but how few confront themselves with it, or lay open all the soul to all its scrutiny? This is what is wanted, in order to a right appreciation of time and eternity, in their respective claims upon our attention. That vague sense of divine observation, which allows a man to take liberties under the eye of God that he durst not venture upon before the eye of the world, is very little better than an actual denial of omniscience. Even that sense of it, which leaves the conscience at ease, except when open sin is perpetrating, is but half a recognition of the divine scrutiny. It extends to the whole frame of our spirit, and to all the secrets of our heart, and to the exact kind and degree of attention we give to divine things. It looks to the meaning of our words, to the spirit of our forms, to the motives of our actions, to the centers of our affections, and to the precise character of our desires, as well as to our practical doings and prevailing temper. It is a discerner of the thoughts and intents of the heart, that, like a two-edged sword, penetrates even to the joints and marrow of our moral frame, dividing them asunder, and laying bare the whole hidden man of the heart. This is omniscience. Nothing is hid from it, or overlooked by it. It also remembers as imperishably, as it marks impartially. It never mistakes, and never wearies. Now, we do not like this minute and everlasting observation. It is both too rigid and too constant for our taste. We may not exactly dispute nor despise it; but we are very willing to forget it, and very ready, when it is forced upon our notice, to try to persuade ourselves, that we could do nothing else, if we were to attend to our hearts as it requires. For, who has not got up a case against such watchfulness as the omniscience of God seems to call for? Thus we exaggerate its claims into an impossibility, and then excuse ourselves for neglecting them. This is a very paltry subterfuge. We are afraid to deny that God keeps His eye constantly upon us, and yet we venture to affirm that we cannot be expected to keep our eye constantly on Him. This, however, is not true. It is, of course, quite true, that we cannot be always thinking of God, nor forever on the strain to keep every thought, feeling, and desire, up to the mark of a high spirituality; but this is not what He expects. He does not apply the measure of an angel to the abilities of a man. He regards business done in his fear with as much complacency as the devotion which preceded and followed it, in the habits of a pious man. He would reckon perpetual musing no homage to Him, even if His own character were the subject of it, if the muser loved meditation because he disliked labor. Idle men, however absorbed about divine things, are as far from coming up to God's standard of a Christian, as active men who care nothing about divine things.

God exercises his omniscience for the on-carrying of the ordinary duties of life, as well as for the enforcement of the duties of godliness. He looks after work as well as worship. It is, therefore, sheer hypocrisy, or utter silliness, to pretend impossibilities, when He calls on us to do and endure, "as seeing Him who is invisible." God has a practical object in view as much as any other father, who looks well after his family. He does not look at every thing in our hearts and lives for the sake of looking, nor only that He might find fault, nor chiefly because He will bring all things into judgment at the last day. The minuteness and constancy of his observations are for our good on all days, and not for evil even on that day. No!

Omniscience is not trying how much it can get up against us at the judgment-seat, but how much it can keep down the clauses of our indictment there. It is not collecting evidence with a view to our condemnation, but for the express purpose of rousing us, by a sight of all that it has seen, to seek that robe of righteousness in which we may be acquitted when the thrones are set for judgment. I wish I could say something on this point which you could never forget, nor lose sight of again; for I strongly suspect that the omniscience of God is regarded as a jealous spy, rather than as a watchful friend. This is very base! For, next to the gift of a Savior and a Sanctifier, the greatest proof that God is love, is, that He searcheth the heart, and trieth the reins, and thus acquaints Himself with all our ways. This assertion should not surprise you at all. It is no paradox nor pretense struck out to meet an emergency, or to evade a difficulty. I know, indeed, too well, that omniscience wears a repulsive and prying aspect to the generality; but I know equally well, that they have not studied its revealed character or design. They do not think of it at all, but when it stands in their way as an angel with a drawn sword, holding them back from their sins and follies. It is thus they come to regard it rather as an enemy than a friend.

Perhaps, you have never seen any thing amiable or pleasing in this perfection of God. Perhaps, you even doubt whether His sleepless omniscience could be construed, by any ingenuity, into a proof of paternal love. Or, if you do not altogether question this, you do question the possibility of bringing you to love it as much as you now fear it. That you think impossible in your own case. You do not even see how any man could really delight in having the eye of God forever fixed on all his movements and emotions. There seems something irksome and embarrassing in such observations, whatever were its motives. I bring out these suspicions, because I know they are in the heart. I am not suggesting, by thus embodying them in words, ideas or feelings which you have been strangers to until now. You never have loved the omniscience of God, nor allowed yourself to suppose that you ever could love it. For, why else are you surprised, that I call it a lovely attribute? You too, however, would think it so, if your heart were thoroughly set upon an immediate personal interest in the great salvation. Did that absorb your spirit in deep solicitude—in fervent prayer—in insatiable desire for acceptance with God through the blood of the Lamb, you would be delighted to remember that an omniscient eye saw all your desires, and examined all your feelings. You would not for worlds have it otherwise, were you intent upon true repentance towards God, and on true faith towards our Lord Jesus Christ. You would be so willing to repent and believe aright, and so anxious to be sure that you did so, and so afraid of mistaking at all in a matter of such infinite importance, that you would actually rejoice in the pleasing fact of an omniscience which marked all your sincerity, and understood you better than you could express or explain yourself.

"Thou God, seest me," will be one of the sweetest considerations that ever passed through your mind, when your mind tries to pour all its strength into fervent prayers for mercy and grace. Then, the eye of God, like the cross of Christ, will appear to you "altogether lovely;" and you will appeal forever after, when examining your own love to God, as Peter did, "Lord, thou knowest all things, thou knowest that I love thee."

Thus, it is not impossible to delight in the omniscience of God. It becomes an anchor to the soul, when the soul cannot find words nor tears to express its concern for salvation. But you say, "How will it appear when this absorbing concern subsides? It may be very pleasing whilst all the soul is concentrated upon obtaining the hope of salvation; but, when that hope is obtained, and both worlds resume their proper place in the heart, how will Omniscience commend itself to the heart then?" I will not evade this question by insinuating that you want to make some provision for doing, thinking, and feeling, at times, what you would not venture on if you could not forget the eye of God. Take care, however, that there be no lurking design of this kind at the bottom of the question. I suspect none, but you do well to suspect yourself.

It is, then, the constancy of divine observation, under ordinary circumstances, that seems irksome or unpleasant to you. You cannot see how it could be a daily source of pleasure to a man who has to stand the tear and wear of the business of life; so many thoughts and feelings must pass through his mind inevitably, and the majority of them must be so worldly, that nothing but pain or shame could well arise from closing the day by a solemn review of what Omniscience had noticed and marked in the course of it. This is plausible. It is, however, untrue. In order to see this, you have only to ask yourself—Would it not give me pleasure, if God did not notice the frame of my mind during the bustle of the day, nor during the hours of relaxation? Suppose His eye were upon me only when I was in the closet and the sanctuary, would I like that better than its following me everywhere? This would, indeed, relieve me from some embarrassment: but how would it place me, as to safety, during the interval that the eye of God was not upon me? I need its watchfulness at all times, and everywhere, however I may dislike its scrutiny. Might there not, however, spring up some thought, feeling, or passion, whilst He lost sight of my heart through the day, which would prove fatal to my principles or character, before He renewed his observation at night? Might not my mind take some turn, or get some bias, whilst He left it to itself, which would prevent my return to the closet or the sanctuary? Besides, would Satan slumber even if God slept?

"Ay, there's the rub!"

We do not know what we wish, when we desire to be less noticed by Omniscience. Were "He that keepeth Israel" to "slumber or sleep," the enemy of souls would ruin our souls in the intervals of divine watchfulness. Omniscience is watchfulness as well as scrutiny. Whilst, therefore, I readily grant, that both pain and shame must accompany a review of the thoughts and feelings of any day, I deny that nothing else better can accompany it. I challenge contradiction when I affirm that it is both sweet and soothing to discover that however the world may have divided the heart from God, and the things of time and sense diverted it from eternity, they have not been allowed to alienate it entirely, nor to turn it against religion. It is, indeed, humiliating to come home from the toils and turmoil of life, deadened, distracted, and carnalized; but, bad as this is, it is better than coming home seared in conscience, or perverted in judgment. And I defy any man to prove that this might not happen, if God did not interpose checks upon the tendencies of the heart, and counteraction upon the influence of Satan and the world. It is not, therefore, only for the sake of marking what is evil in the trains of our thoughts and feelings, that God keeps his eye upon them all; but, chiefly, that He may stop them at all the points where vain thoughts might become vicious, and bad feelings reprobate.

I tell you, therefore, in plain terms, that had God taken less notice of your heart than He has done, it would have been harder than it is, and even "past feeling," long ago. Now this you would not like. This you deprecate. You cannot, therefore, dislike now (as you did) the all-seeing and all-searching eye of God. It has kept the eye of your understanding somewhat open to the truth and importance of eternal things, and the eye of your conscience from confounding evil with good. Is not that a lovely attribute, then, which thus condescends to watch the workings of the mind, and the effect of temptations and circumstances upon the mind, that it may interpose when prejudice would ripen into enmity, and distaste into settled aversion, for divine things? Do your views of Omniscience, and your feelings towards it, begin to alter a little now? Do you see that more can be said to endear it than you supposed at first? Well, I am only skirting the edges and skimming the surface of its grace and glory. "These are a part of its ways;" but only a small portion of them is known when all this is understood. For, what think you of the grace of Omniscience, in so watching over the movements of the public mind, as to maintain a tone of thought and feeling, upon the whole, favorable to personal piety? I mean, that you may be pious without periling life or reputation, although the great bulk of mankind are still ungodly. This is no accident, nor a small advantage. Now, it is by searching all hearts that God can turn all hearts, like rivers, into any channel He pleases. Did he not keep His eye upon the spirit of the age, and thus regulate its passions, there is enough both of infidelity and popery in it to rekindle the fires of martyrdom, and turn the finger of scorn into the fist of cruelty.

4

On Manly Realizations of Final Judgment

We shall never do well in the service of God until we act in all things with an express regard to the final "Well done," of the Judge. We shall neither be good nor faithful servants if we do not set our hearts upon His commendation, as well as upon His acquittal at the judgment-seat. Indeed, he will acquit none whom He cannot commend also for something. To none will He say, "Come, ye blessed, inherit the kingdom," but to those to whom He can say first, "Well done." Where He cannot say of something, "Well done, ye blessed," He will say, "Depart, ye cursed." Thus it will be at the last day exactly as the Savior said on the first and last days of His public ministry on earth: only those who "have done good shall come forth unto the resurrection of life: they that have done evil shall come forth unto the resurrection of damnation." John 5:29. There will be no well-being then, where there has been no well-doing now. This solemn fact does not affect all minds alike: but it brings out, whenever it is brought home, both the secrets and the real state of all hearts. It is a glass in which every man sees at once his own character and disposition. At the first glance it sets the clever compromiser to try all his theological dexterity, in order to evade or neutralize the startling truth. He is not inclined to do much in the service of God, nor to do well the little he attempts; and therefore he tries to perplex the question about well-doing. "Men are not saved (he says) by doing good, nor for doing well; and therefore it is very legal to set them such a task, as trying to deserve the commendation of the Judge. No one could merit that. He is no Christian, who imagines that he deserves to be welcomed into heaven by the 'Well done' of the Judge. All must enter the kingdom as sinners saved entirely by free grace. Christians must not, indeed, do evil when they can avoid it; but neither must they do good for the sake of a reward." Thus the compromiser perplexes the question, and perils his soul upon a quibble; for it is a quibble to say that it would be legal, or self-righteous, to do the work of faith or the labor of love well. Trying to do them well is the true and sure way of not depending upon them. He who does best, or tries how well he can do, in the service of God, is sure to feel most that he cannot merit salvation. Accordingly, the holiest Christians are always the humblest; and the most exemplary in character, the most frequent at the cross, and most fervent at the mercy-seat. Theory may say, that the man who is doing little, and nothing well, would be oftenest and humblest there: but all experience proves the contrary. They are anything but very prayerful, who are very inconsistent in their habits or spirit. They glory least in the cross, who run least for the crown. This is the fact, whatever the theory may be.

None feel or confess themselves entire debtors to grace and dependents on Christ, so much as those who do and try most to resemble the Savior in character, and to glorify Him by devotedness. And all this is only what might be expected. Sound theory, as well as sober fact, lead to this conclusion. For, how could he be expected to pray most or much, who does nothing else well? He is not likely to love prayer, who dislikes practical godliness. He has, indeed, most occasion to pray much, but he has, naturally and inevitably, least inclination, because least hope of success. Besides, it is in religion, as it is in the intercourse of life: the man who is all the day long neglecting the advice of his best friend, will not court his friend's company at night, for many nights together. He will soon weary of being alone with him, and invent as many excuses for not meeting him at night, as for not acting on his advice by day.

And, at length, sheer shame will keep him away altogether, unless sheer necessity drive him back. So it is in religion: nothing is so irksome to an idle or inconsistent professor as being alone with God in the closet. There, he is completely out of his element. In fact, he dare not stay long enough upon his knees to go into his own case before God. It will not bear looking at, and therefore he hushes it up, and hurries away. Not so, however, with the man who tries to do well through the day. He is not afraid of his closet at night. He is, indeed, ashamed of his failures and imperfections, even when he has done best; but it is a shame that draws him into his closet; that endears his evening interview with God in secret; because there, he regains the hope of pardon, and thus renews his spiritual strength for an attempt to do better to-morrow.

There are, however, some truly pious persons, who, although they are deeply afraid of doing evil, are also conscientiously afraid of calling or considering their good, "well-doing." They have no hope—no idea—of hearing the "Well done" of the Judge applied to any thing they do or try. The very utmost they venture to look for is escape from condemnation. A silent, or even an unseen admission into heaven, would more than satisfy them. If only allowed to "steal in," however unnoticed, it would be enough for them: so deeply sensible are they of their utter unworthiness. Now this is a fine spirit, so far as it makes Christ "all and all," in salvation. But whilst it does honor to Him as a Priest it does not do justice to Him as a King. It is the only right spirit in reference to His cross; but it is not so right towards His scepter. He feels and takes a higher interest in all who love Him than to provide only for their admission into heaven. That would not satisfy Him, however it might content them. More than acquittal is laid up for all that "love His appearing:" a crown of righteousness will be given to them. He will honor as well as own them. This should not be overlooked. It is not humility to think of nothing but bare escape at the judgment-seat. Were there, indeed, nothing more provided or promised, it would be pride, yes, arrogance, to wish for any thing beyond mere pardon. But as Christ has "prepared a place," and promised "a crown" to all His followers, it is their duty to look for both, and to prepare themselves for both. This would produce greater humility than the mere hope of safety calls forth; for if it bow my soul in adoring wonder to think of being allowed a place of safety at the right hand of the Judge; if I feel that I could not stand there, however unnoticed without being overpowered with a sense of my own unworthiness and of His grace; how much more would all these humble emotions prevail and abide in my soul, were I to anticipate a welcome—a smile —a kind word or look from Him! The thought of that, dissolves the soul in humility, as well as "in wonder, love, and praise." Why is this fact so much overlooked by some who love both humility and holiness? They certainly judge ill, however well they mean, in thus looking for less than the Savior has promised. Their difficulty, I apprehend, lies here: they cannot connect His "Well dome," with ordinary well-doing. It must, they think, be confined to the extraordinary well-doing of public champions in the cause of God. They can connect it with martyrs, missionaries, faithful ministers, and a few eminently devoted Christians; but with their own poor and private well-doing, they never think of linking it. That seems to them altogether out of question and of character.

This is, however, quite a mistake. It is not thus that the Savior estimates service done to him. We look only or chiefly at splendid and public well-doing; at efforts and sacrifices which tell powerfully upon the world and the church, and which draw down tokens of the divine approbation now, that amount to pledges and preludes of commendation when the thrones shall be set for judgment. But, although we are not wrong in thus attaching the chief importance to public men and measures, so far as new triumphs of the cross are wanted and to be won, we are not right when we forget even the humblest trophies of its old triumphs. They are quite as much connected with sustaining the glory of Christ, as the others are with extending it. It is the worth of private Christians that bears out public men in maintaining that the gospel is worthy of all acceptation. It is the prayers of private Christians that bear up the spirits and hopes of ministers, missionaries, and philanthropists.

Were not poor Christians cheerful, and suffering Christians patient, and bereaved Christians resigned, and tempted Christians steadfast, public champions could not appeal to facts when enforcing the claims of God and godliness; for although their claims do not rest upon the number nor the excellence of private Christians, still these are the living proofs and demonstrations that they are well founded. Thus, the public servants of Christ are enabled to do well by the well-doing of his private friends. The great things attempted and achieved for His glory, by extraordinary men, are upheld by the prayers, the character, and the spirit of ordinary Christians, and therefore His "Well done" is just as sure in the case of the latter, as in that of the former. Both are but instruments by which He works; and, perhaps, the silent influence of private piety has not less to do with His glory, than the commanding influence of public "standard-bearers." It is, therefore, a pity that such facts are overlooked.

The poorest, in common with the wealthiest Christian, and the plainest in common with the most talented or eloquent, have it in their power to secure the commendation of the Judge: for prayer as well as preaching, character as well as gifts, patience as well as enterprise, promote His glory. Were this well understood by all the humble followers of the Lamb, they would do more and better in His service than ever they did. It would not lead them to attach too much importance to themselves. It would not set them to trace out the precise degree of their own consequence in the church on earth, nor to guess at their place in the church in heaven. The greatest dare not yield to that temptation, whilst looking forward to the judgment-seat, and the least would never think of such calculations. No man can become consequential or self-important by acting as one who is preparing to give an account at the great white throne of the deeds done in the body.

Were there, however, even some positive danger of being betrayed into self-complacency by trying how good an account we could give "at last," there is far more danger in not trying. That may betray us into sloth, heedlessness, or even into Antinomian-presumption; a spirit not so easily "cast out," as self-complacency. Accordingly, whilst you have seen many professed Christians too worldly, slothful, and self-indulgent, you never saw an exemplary Christian pluming himself on the prospect of being able to give his "account with joy, and not with grief," nor puffed up with the hope of being found "in peace on that day."

This is now the point at which I may safely venture to say, that there is a sense in which Christians attach too little importance to themselves as Christians. Had they more respect for themselves, as members of God's family on earth, and as heirs of his kingdom in heaven, they would act better than they do. Self-respect is a very different thing from self-importance. It is even a security against self-importance. A Christian, who respects himself as a Christian, cannot be consequential or assuming. He has too little respect for himself, if he can give himself airs of importance, or carry himself at all proudly. Whenever any man does so, it is not his Christianity, not his hopes, nor his principles, that he respects; but his talents, his taste, his property, or his power: the very least things in his character as a Christian. All vaporing, and ostentation, and assumption take their stand, not upon the measure of grace a man has, but on the measure of gifts, money, or influence he possesses. You never hear a Christian boasting of his grace or holiness. The men who would say to others, "Stand aside, for I am holier than you," are Pharisees, who have little or no dependence on grace. In like manner, all who plume themselves on being special favorites of Heaven, and despise others as non-elect, pay, of all men, the least respect to the grace they pretend to have received. They either turn into licentiousness, or employ it as an excuse for idleness.

When, therefore, I speak of a private Christian respecting himself as a partaker of the grace of God, I mean what you mean, when you say of ministers that they ought to have such a respect for their ministerial character and sacred office, as to be above all meanness, foppishness, and frivolity. You expect and demand that they should "be clean, who bear the vessels of the Lord;" that they who watch for souls should watch as those who have to "give an account" of the souls committed to their charge; that they who are entrusted with the gospel should live the gospel, as well as love and preach it. Well; if this argument is valid and cogent, it holds equally good in the case of private Christians. Those who eat and drink of the vessels of the Lord, as well as those who "bear" them should respect their own character as "the sacramental host of God."

Paul felt this, and told them, "Ye cannot be partakers of the Lord's table, and of the table of devils." Those, also, who deem their souls worthy of ministerial watchfulness, and thus respect them, should respect them enough to bestow on them such personal watchfulness as shall prevent surprise and confusion at the judgment-seat. My meaning will be still better understood when I say, that I am pleading for nothing but the single and simple duty of Christians to regard themselves in the same light as God regards them; to treat themselves as He treats them; to think of themselves as He speaks of them. Now, God speaks of all true believers, however weak or obscure, as His children, His heritage, His temples, His jewels. These titles are not empty names, nor idle compliments. He means what he says: He feels what He professes. Thus, then, God respects them, and thus they should respect themselves: those of them who do not, do wrong.

True, many of them are afraid to regard themselves as the children of God. They are not sure of their adoption or conversion. The only thing they are quite sure of is, that their hearts are set upon being "the children of God, through faith in Jesus Christ." That, however, they do desire and seek after with great solicitude and deep humility. Now, such ought to know and believe, (for they are expressly told the fact by God Himself) that they are His children. They welcome Christ; and to all who receive Him as their Prophet, Priest, and King, God gives "power," that is, warrant or liberty, to regard themselves as the sons and daughters of the Lord God Almighty. They really are so, whether they venture to do so or not. They gain nothing, but lose much, by not doing so; for, by thus leaving their case uncertain and undefined, they are forever laying anew the foundation of piety, instead of building up the fabric of it.

I would be the last to speak harshly, or to think meanly, of those who are afraid to regard themselves as the children of God. I think far more highly of many of them than I do of any who despise the doubting, or who pretend to be superior to all doubts and fears. I cannot, however, shut my eyes to the melancholy fact, that in consequence of leaving it unsettled from year to year whether they are believers or not, not a few fall into the habit of acting, which is like anything rather than like preparing for the judgment-seat of Christ. They do nothing very bad; but they do nothing very good, well. It seems accident, rather than design or effort, when they resist a temptation, or get honorably through a difficulty, or keep their good from being evil spoken of. Somehow, they are seldom to be calculated on. Their best habits, like their hopes, are as changeable as the wind. They are always getting into dilemmas of credit, temper, or character, and rarely get well out of them. Their word is not to be depended on, nor their version of reports safe to be repeated. They are, in a word, a strange jumble of good, bad, and indifferent, which no candid man can altogether despise, and no conscientious man vindicate. If they have any piety, it is not manly.

Here, then, is the consequence of not acting with an express regard to the "Well dome" of the Judge: the oversight prevents well-doing, and brings the mind and conscience into that blunted state which leads to perpetual blundering and compromising, even in things that are easily well done. Now we have seen that the final commendations from the throne will not be restricted to splendid doings, nor to heroic sufferings in the service of God; and that good ordinary men, as well as good extraordinary men, may be counted worthy of public honor at the last day. You, therefore, have no excuse for not trying to do well. It is imperative, because it is not possible through grace. Grace is both ability and obligation to do well. If these hints throw any light on this often mystified subject, the best use you can make of them, in the first instance, is to try to do some one thing well; for trying how well you can perform one duty is the true way of acquiring a taste and habit for doing your best in all duties; indeed, you will do nothing uniformly nor perseveringly in the service of God, until you set yourself to do something as well as you possibly can; and that you will not attempt, until you set the Judge before you.

The praise of men will not inspire well-doing in the service of God for any length of time; nor will legal principles ever lead to many good works. Those who work for salvation do least in obeying, and worst in suffering, the will of God. They, of all men, "make void the law" most, who seek to be justified by the works of the law, instead of the finished work of Christ. This is a remarkable fact. Can you account for it? Look at it again. All who regard salvation as the reward or the result of good works are least "zealous of good works;" whereas, all who have no more dependence on the moral law for salvation, than on the "laws of the Medes and Persians," are fond of the divine law as a rule of life, just in proportion to the strength of their dependence on grace. How is this? It might be expected, surely, that the man who stakes his eternal safety on good works would abound and abide in well-doing, far more than the man who has no dependence on them. But all experience contradicts this expectation. Well-doing prevails most amongst those who seek all their well-being, for time and eternity, in the finished work of Christ.

The fact is, concern about salvation sits very lightly upon the minds of those who prefer the law to the gospel. They care little and think less about the matter. It is not from any love to the works of the law that they prefer it to the gospel; but because they can play it off as a plausible excuse for neglecting the claims of grace. Were law as much and as often pressed upon their consciences as gospel is, they would show equal enmity of heart to it. Instead, therefore, of there being reason to expect that they would obey it best, who trust to it most, all the real reason of the case is on the other side. The generality of them care little about the salvation which they talk of trusting to the law for; and thus their good works come naturally to be as few as their concern for their soul is feeble. And then, as God does not help any man to obey the law who neglects Christ and grace, it is only what might rationally be expected, that even those who try to do well on legal principles should fail very much; for, having no strength of their own, and no aid from the Spirit of God, how could they succeed? God will no more help a man to save himself than He would help a man to ruin himself, now that Christ has suffered and ascended as the only Mediator. God will not displace nor dishonor Him to enable any man to obtain justification by the law.

On the other hand, it is only what might be expected, (if Scripture be allowed to guide expectation) that those should obey most and best who rely on Christ alone for salvation. The tendency of their hope must not be judged by the abstract principle—that the exclusion of the law from all place and part in justifying must exclude it from all place in sanctification. That does not follow either in logic or in probability. The real question is not, "how will a man obey the law, who has no dependence on it for salvation?" but, how will a man obey the law who is redeemed from the curse of it, and thus has no occasion to hate or dread its sanctions? How is he likely to love it, upon whose heart the Spirit of God is writing it? What may be naturally expected from an emaciated slave, when he is adopted as a beloved son? These are the real tests of the real tendencies of a "good hope through grace." God can help, and does help, such a man to obey.

Well-doing in obedience must not be left, however, to depend upon the holy tendencies of gracious principles. It must be both "under law to Christ," and influenced by the judgment-seat of Christ. It will not be fully under law to Christ until it is also under a full sense of accountability to him. He must be recognized and revered as our Judge, if we would habitually or impartially obey Him as our Lawgiver. This remark will enable me to explain to you still further, and more clearly, why many who mean well in the service of God do not act so well as they ought and wish. They bring their conduct to the test of the present mercy seat, more than to the test of the future judgment-seat of Christ. I do not mean that they think too often, or too much, how their conduct during the day will affect their hopes, their peace, or their spirits at the throne of grace at night; but, that they think too seldom how the tenor of their life will look at the throne of judgment. It is this oversight that betrays and weakens them. Their recollection through the day that they must appear before the throne of grace at night to review their conduct, and give in their confession to God, has a fine influence upon them. It operates both as a check and a charm against many temptations; for they know well how the doings of the day will tell upon the devotions of the evening. They can see pretty clearly, even from amidst all the bustle of the world, how certain actions, tempers, and pursuits, will affect their composure in the closet. Not all the din and dust of worldly things can blind them to the solemn fact, that there is a line of conduct which if they overstep they will be unfitted for and afraid of prayer.

It is delightful, also, to trace the sweet and holy influence which the prospect of having to appear at the sacrament has upon the well-doing of Christians. It both leads and compels them to pause often, in the course of the month, to ask themselves, "How will this line of conduct—this frame of spirit—this ascendant habit, affect my enjoyment at the sacramental table? I shall be expected there, as a matter of course, by my pastor and friends. My absence would create surprise at home: it might excite suspicion elsewhere. I must not absent myself! And yet, how can I appear at the altar of God, if I give way to a wrong spirit or to irregular habits?" Here, also, the realization of the sacramental tribunal stimulates to well-doing, and restrains from ill-doing. Thus the daily interview with God in secret, and the monthly commemoration of the love of Christ in public, aid all the good principles of the heart, and operate as an antidote against the ensnaring influence of the world.

Now, the man who can bring his conduct to the test of those devotional tribunals, can do more. He who is thus eagle-eyed to discern how all that is wrong will embarrass his hopes and embitter his enjoyments there, is equally capable of testing his spirit and habits at a higher tribunal. He must appear at the judgment-seat of Christ, and therefore ought to act with as much reference to it as to the mercy-seat of the altar. This, however, is not generally done; and the consequence is, well-doing is not so uniform or spirited as it might be.

I have thus tried your patience, no doubt, in leading you round and round this subject, without having once gone fully up to its solemnities or glories, or grappled with its chief difficulties. I have done so purposely. I want you to see, through the medium of others, how your own heart and conscience stand affected to the grand principle of acting with an express view to the commendation of the Judge. He will not call that well done, which is ill done or left undone. He will deal with "deeds and works," on the great day of reckoning, and render to every man "according to his works and deeds." To them who, by "patient continuance in well-doing, seek for glory, honor, and immortality, He will give eternal life;" but "tribulation and anguish" will be the doom of "every soul of man that doeth evil." Romans ii. 6–10.

Say not, "Who then can be saved?" Say rather, "How easy Christ has made it for us to do well!" This is the fact, whatever may be your feelings on the subject. I have already shown you that well-doing is both practicable and profitable in any sphere of life. Christ taught this, when He commended the "widow's mite," as well as Mary's "box of costly ointment." He taught it, when he said that "a cup of cold water" given for His sake should no more lose its reward, than the sacrifice of life or property. He exemplified it, when He promised the dying thief an entrance into Paradise; for although the only well-doing he had time or opportunity for was to give a public testimony to the Savior's innocence, when His friends forsook, and His enemies insulted him, even that was publicly rewarded. It deserves special notice, also, that, in his account of the last judgment, He identifies himself with the poor and the afflicted members of God's family, as well as commends the benevolent, who visited and relieved them. "Verily, I say unto you, inasmuch as ye have done it unto one of the least of these my brethren, ye have done it unto me." Matthew 25:40. Here, not only is relief to one reckoned well-doing, in order that all who have but little to spare, may do well, in common with those who have much; but even those Christians who got what was thus given for the sake of Christ are commended by implication; for, by owning them as his brethren in poverty and tribulation, it is implied that their patience, for His name's sake, was reckoned well-doing on their part.

Thus all may share in the "Well done" of the Judge, who are willing to do well, according to their ability. Nothing, therefore, is more unfounded than the suspicion that the judgment-seat cannot be realized without fear and suspense. Christ teaches no such doctrine to his followers. The gospel calls on them to "lift up their heads" in prospect of His second coming. They are, indeed, taught also, to prepare for it by watchfulness and diligence that they may be "found of Him in peace on that day;" but they are not taught to look forward to his coming with terror or distrust. None who honor Him as a Savior need fear to meet Him as a Judge. Only those who dislike well-doing for His name's sake are in danger from His sentence.

Were these facts more frequently inculcated, when the last judgment is described from the pulpit and the press, more good would be done than usually results from terrific appeals to

"A God in grandeur,
And a world on fire."

It is by far too common to speak and think most of the dread solemnities of the last day. When that grand assize of the universe is the subject, imagination embodies all its darkest visions; eloquence speaks in all its deepest tones; zeal pleads with all its heart-thrilling remonstrance; pity weeps big and burning tears; and thus the preacher and hearers, however pious, become so absorbed by scenes of conflagration and horror that both resign themselves to fear and trembling whilst the appeal lasts, and only recover their composure as the flaming vision fades away or is forgotten. I am not finding fault with such preaching. It is often wanted, in order to rouse the righteous, as well as to arrest the wicked. He trifles with souls, and perils his own soul, who does not empanel, from time to time, all souls at the judgment-seat, and make its thunders reverberate the threatening, "The soul that sinneth shall die." This is, however, but one part of "the revelation of the righteous judgment of God."

"Come, ye blessed," will sound as loud from the throne as, "Depart, ye cursed;" and, therefore, it ought to be as frequently repeated in the pulpit, and as much employed to promote hope and composure amongst the well-doing, as the latter is to alarm the idle and the ungodly. Wherever this is not done, there will be a spirit of bondage to the fear of judgment that will not tempt Christians not to think of it often; for no man will think oftener than he can help of what only terrifies him.

Again, therefore, I say, there is no need for terror on the part of the well-doing followers of Christ. The judgment seat will not disannul the pardons obtained at the mercy seat. Conscientious obedience will be as surely owned at the former, as fervent prayer is answered at the latter. The inevitable imperfections of duty will no more prevent it from being accepted as well-doing, at last, than the imperfections of devotion hinder it from being accepted as prayer now. A Christian, therefore, who is doing his best from right principles, has no more occasion to fear the worst on that day, than to despair of success at the mercy-seat, because he is ashamed of his own imperfect prayers. He is not ashamed of them without reason; but still he is sure that they are not insincere, not heartless, nor formal. He can appeal to the heart-searching God that his cry for mercy and grace "goeth not out of feigned lips."

Accordingly, whilst all his hope of success in prayer hinges exclusively upon the intercession of Christ, this testimony of his own conscience helps him to rely on that intercession, and to look with some composure to the throne of grace. Now, thus also he is warranted to look forward to the great white throne of judgment; never fearing the worst, whilst conscientiously trying to do his best.

I am well aware how the familiar phrase, "doing my best," is both vulgarly and viciously employed by many. It is the language of the ignorant, when they speak of the gospel as a provision for making up the defects of their own obedience from the merits of Christ. It is the excuse of the slothful and the heedless when they would palliate sin by an appeal to the force of circumstances, which, they say, prevented them from doing better. It is also a standard which every man may vary to suit himself, if he be so unprincipled as to call anything "his best." I see and feel all this; but still, I will not give up the phrase because many pervert it. It is as emphatic as it is familiar. To the well-disposed it is a fine rule of well-doing. It recognizes both their obligations by law, and their ability by grace, and thus throws them upon their best principles in doing their best for God.

How, then, does this matter appear to you now? How do you feel affected towards "patient continuance in well-doing? Do deal honestly with yourself on this point. Not to like well-doing is virtually to say of Christ, "We will not have this man to reign over us;" and to such He will say, as the books are opened on the throne, "Bring out these mine enemies, that would not have me to reign over them, and destroy them in My sight." You will not, surely, risk this fearful threatening! Even if you still feel some reluctance to try how well you can do, you cannot, in the face of this warning, deem it safe to indulge that reluctance. Take care, however, not to wink at, nor to hush up the question; for all the probability of your salvation turns upon your willingness to serve Christ.

Until you are willing to do well, you are not only strangers to Christ and grace, but also setting them both at defiance. He died for you, that you should be zealous of good works. The grace which bringeth salvation brings it teaching us to live soberly, righteously, and godly, in the present world. They are, therefore, both the enemies of the cross, and the perverters of grace, whose god is their belly, or who mind earthly things. The end of both is "destruction," whatever be their creed, or their profession.

5

Manly Realizations of Invisible Things

When the Roman army besieged Jerusalem, the temple was, of course, the last place to yield or open. Never was any place so defended. Mass after mass of the Jews throw themselves between the soldiers and the gates of the temple, daring and defying death. It was literally over hills of carnage that the Roman legions forced their way into the Jewish temple. When they had thus made an entrance, nothing, it is said, surprised them so much as the utter absence of all images. In their own temples at Rome, images of the gods smiled or frowned from every point and pillar; but, in the temple of Jerusalem, neither without nor within the veil, could they see any sign, symbol, shadow, or trace of the form or person of the God of Israel. Emblems of His grace and glory emblazoned the whole building, from the Holy of Holies to the court of the Gentiles; but, no graven nor sculptured image of Jehovah was to be seen.

Now, if Judaism was thus singular from its entire want of all visible images of the true God, Christianity is still more singular: for it has no visible emblem even of the glory of God, nor any miraculous symbol of His grace. All the chief objects of Christian faith are absolutely unseen. The Father of the Christian church is invisible: her Redeemer is invisible: her Comforter invisible; her ministering spirits invisible: her throne of grace invisible: even her future heaven is invisible. This prevailing and permanent invisibility of all the supreme objects of our faith and hope is a surprising fact in itself, however custom may have rendered us familiar with it. Accordingly, when it is pointed out to us, we do wonder that a religion which promises so much should show so little.

There must be some wise and weighty reason for thus concealing from the eye entirely what is so openly revealed to the understanding. God could easily appear annually on the circle of the heavens, or open occasionally the heaven of heavens to our view. He has done greater things for our world than this. It is not, therefore, from any want of love or solicitude for our souls that He keeps himself and heaven invisible. It must be because we could not sustain the "great sight" in the present state of our faculties. Those who remember how Moses quaked on Sinai, and how John fell as dead in Patmos, will not doubt this. We may, however, inquire with perfect freedom—what is it that "makes up" to us for this strict and standing, and even studied invisibility of all the chief objects of faith and hope?

Now, it is the eternity of their duration that makes up for the invisibility of their character. If they are all "unseen"—they are all "eternal." This is the compensation; and it is an ample, a noble compensation, when duly considered. Let us prepare to consider it duly, by marking the contrast between visible and invisible objects. All things which are but temporal are visible. The very beasts are allowed to see the whole range of temporal things. It is not thought worth while to veil evanescent and temporary objects. They are all good enough to be worth showing; but none of them good enough to be worth concealing under the veil of mystery or of futurity. Thus temporal things, being no part of the soul's portion, are all thrown open to our bodily senses. None of them being everlasting, all of them are forever seen. All things which are visible are but temporal. Nothing earthly is eternal. Were there, however, any visible things eternal also, even they would be but temporal to us, because we ourselves are mortal. Were all earthly things everlasting in themselves, they would be only temporary to us: for we cannot last, even if they could endure. But none of them will endure forever. They are all destined to perish. The earth will be burnt up, and the very heavens pass away with a great noise. All that is now seen, even of the works of creation, will be seen no more, when the Angel swears that time shall be no more. And if the material works of God shall not outlast time, nor outlive man, of course the works of man will perish too.

Thus there is nothing visible that is deemed worthy of preservation through eternity: nothing fit to be transferred from earth to heaven. No building, however sublime; no book, however wise; no science, however profound; no art, however noble; no ornament, however splendid; no amusement, however pleasant, will be spared from "the wreck of matter and crash of worlds." Palaces and temples will perish in common with huts; cabinets and treasuries along with trifles; and libraries with the flowers of the field; for when God burns the book of nature, He will not save the volumes of learning or genius. What a wreck is coming on temporal things. Wreck! The coming conflagration will not leave even "a wreck behind."

You have listened to me on this subject. Now listen to an apostle: "Seeing all these things shall be burnt up, what manner of persons ought ye to be in all holy conversation and godliness?" 2 Peter 3:11.

Do you regret the utter and entire annihilation of any of these things? Is there any gem of art, or of science, or of genius, that you would wish spared, and transferred to heaven? If you do, I share not this feeling with you. I rejoice in the utter-ness and eternity of the destruction, because it will destroy all the associations of vain and unholy thoughts and feelings, which are now connected with temporal things: for, when forever out of being, they will be forever out of mind.

Besides, heaven needs none of these things to perfect its bliss or glory. The very sun itself is not wanted there; for the Lamb is the light thereof. The universality and eternity of the final ruin tell, therefore, what heaven is: it is a place that can do forever without them all.

Thus happiness, real happiness, must be a very different thing from what we naturally suppose, seeing heaven and eternity fling such scorn upon all earthly good, that they will admit no particle of it amongst invisible things. The things of time and sense cannot deserve so much of our heart and care, seeing they are all to be flung into the furnace of annihilation. It is surely of less consequence than we make it, whether to be rich or poor, seeing we can carry nothing out of the world, and that nothing in it can be brought to heaven or hell.

What, I ask again, what must heaven be, seeing it rejects all earthly joys as useless and worthless to its happiness? This single thought, simple as it is, would bear pondering for months. Also, the covetous and the worldly cannot take their gold into hell with them; nor the intemperate their cups; nor the jovial their jests or songs. Under the solemn and salutary impression of these hints, let us now observe how the eternity of unseen things makes up for their present invisibility. It proves, to demonstration, their infinite superiority to all earthly things. For, were the things which are seen better than what they are; were they even as safe and satisfying as they were before sin cursed and corrupted them; still, as they are only temporal, they are unworthy and unfit to be a portion for souls in eternity. Our spirits require eternal things, if they are to have any suitable portion; so that if unseen things were even fewer and less glorious than they are, the single fact of their being eternal throws into shade and insignificance, so far as the soul is concerned, all temporal things. For, if we are to be as truly happy as we are immortal, we must have immortal sources of happiness. We need everlasting peace, everlasting comforts, everlasting joys; and these the world cannot furnish, even if the joy it gives were perfect.

Were there, therefore, nothing unsatisfying, yea, nothing sinful, yea, nothing dangerous, in an earthly portion, I would denounce it, and renounce it, on the single ground of its short duration. "It is not eternal," ought to repel and prevent our souls from seeking their happiness in this world. "It is eternal," ought to attract and determine us to seek first the kingdom of heaven, even if that kingdom were inferior to this earth. The eternity of unseen things proves their intrinsic excellence. They derive their eternity from an excellence which deserves to be eternal.

The glories of heaven are full and perfect, not because they are everlasting, but they are everlasting because they are perfect. Its crowns are unfading, because they deserve to flourish forever; its mansions un-falling, because they deserve to stand forever; its thrones immoveable, because they deserve to endure forever; its society undying, because it deserves to live forever; its peace imperishable, because it deserves to reign forever; its holiness unchangeable, because it deserves to last forever. For, as all earthly things are temporal, just because they are imperfect, so all heavenly things are eternal, just because they are infinitely perfect.

This is the moral foundation of future happiness. It rests upon the intrinsic and essential moral worth of all its sources; and, therefore, cannot end nor alter, because holiness is its conservative principle. The eternity of unseen things proves the amplitude and perfection of the work of Christ in heaven. When about to ascend there, He said, "I go to prepare a place for you." And ample and glorious that preparation must be, seeing that nothing in all the prepared place will ever require to be altered. What the Savior made heaven when He sat down on the throne, that heaven will remain throughout eternity. Yes; all the unseen things which He has laid up for them that love Him are eternal things. No crown of glory shall ever dim; no palm of victory ever wither; no harp of gold ever break; no fruit of the tree of life ever fail; no fountain of the water of life ever dry; no element or item of celestial bliss ever pass away; but all things continue, like Christ Himself, the same forever. What a work, therefore, was His in heaven.

We judge of His atoning work on earth, by the many sons it will bring to glory, and fit for glory; and thus learn to admire and adore the merits of that death which obtained for them eternal redemption. And thus we should judge; thus we should learn. But let us judge also, and equally well, from the number and eternity of the glories of heaven, the value of that life which He lived there, whilst preparing the place which He opened by his blood. The eternity of unseen things proves the perfection of the sanctifying and ennobling work of the Holy Spirit upon the heirs of heaven. The redeemed will be fully prepared by the

MANLY PIETY IN ITS REALIZATIONS

Spirit to enjoy all that the Savior has prepared for them. There will be nothing in all the eternal weight of glory too high for their minds, or too holy for their taste, or too extensive for their powers. The eternal light of heaven will not be too dazzling for their eyes; nor its eternal worship too constant for their strength; nor its eternal fellowship too wide or too warm for their inclination; but they will be mentally and morally fit for all the bliss and business of heaven, and for an eternity of it all.

This shows us, in some light, what the work of the Holy Spirit is. It will bring up the mind, and the body too, to the lofty height of heaven's highest, purest, and eternal enjoyments. It will run out all the powers and affections of the soul in grand parallel with the whole range of heavenly things. It will harmonize all its tastes and desires, with all the sources of divine happiness; and knit, in everlasting bonds of love, the hearts of all saints to each other, and of all saints and angels together. Oh quench not, grieve not the Holy Spirit, if He has begun this good work in you; for this is the length to which it must be carried on—the length to which He will carry it on, in all the heirs of salvation. We must be made meet for the inheritance of the righteous. And with equal solicitude and solemnity, I beseech and adjure you, if you are stifling and evading your convictions of guilt and danger, to stop. "Resist not the Holy Spirit." What would you think of my conduct, if I were to resist the attraction of heaven's glories as they shine and sound through its open gates? Neglecter of the great salvation, you are resisting more than all this, whilst banishing and evading the strivings of conscience, and the force of truth. You are resisting the love of God—the blood of the Lamb—the drawings of the Spirit. Oh stop— yield; and from this moment stand out no more against the claims of your soul and eternity.

The eternity of unseen things proves how fully the happiness of heaven will arise from fellowship with the Godhead, and conformity to the divine image. I would not venture to give utterance to my sentiments on this subject, did I not suspect that what I had hinted on the eternity of unseen things, may suggest the question, "will there, then, be nothing new added as eternal ages roll on? Will the scene be forever the same?" I meet this thought, not in a speculative spirit, but to throw your mind on the sublime fact, that eternal bliss will flow infinitely more from the presence and image of God, than from the glories of heaven, as a place. As a place, it will be to saints and angels, what it is to God and the Lamb, not the cause of their eternal happiness, nor the chief source of it; but the chief seat of it. The real source of felicity will be the company and communion enjoyed with the Godhead, and that would make a heaven even on earth; or, indeed, anywhere.

As a place, however, heaven is altogether becoming and worthy of the majesty and glory of Jehovah; and as it suits His infinite mind, and will please Him forever, it cannot fail to satisfy forever all His redeemed family. They will no more want nor wish for a new heaven, than for a new Father, a new Redeemer, or a new Comforter. Besides, eternal things are perfect; and pure souls can never tire of perfection; because, as it admits of no change for the better, so they can never wish a change for the worse. There is, therefore, no more reason to regret the unchangeableness of heaven itself, than that God will be the same forever; for it will be forever as unnecessary and impossible to wish a change of scene, society, or service, as to wish the love of God to cool, or the power of God to decay, or the wisdom of God to fail, or the glory of God to diminish.

In thus maintaining that heaven will never be altered, because it cannot be altered for the better, nothing is, however, further from my design than to convey the idea that there will be no new sources of enjoyment as eternity goes on. There may—there most likely will be many; but, whatever they be, they will not displace the old. New eternal things, if such be created, "whilst immortality endures," will all like the old, make and keep God Himself the chief source of happiness to all the armies of heaven.

I want you to see and feel that eternal happiness will and must come from God himself. All the value, and sweetness, and glory of every thing in heaven, will arise from every thing leading and lifting the soul to God, as its center and portion; and thus making Him all and all, even amidst all the splendors of the heaven of heavens. You, are, therefore, duping and deceiving yourself, if you imagine that you may reach heaven without seeking your chief happiness in God here. Those who take no pleasure in Him here, will get none in Him there. Those who dislike to think of God, to pray to Him, or commune with Him, never can dwell with Him.

Will you stop and turn fully from the way that goeth down to the chambers of hell? You cannot bear me to uncover destruction in this way. I cannot bear to see you risking it. You think me harsh for dwelling thus on eternal realities. I think you frantic in neglecting the only Savior from the wrath to come. But, I forgey! This is not a matter between you and me. What I think of you, or you of me, is not worth a thought at this moment.

The God who prepared this hell for Satan and his angels, and who gave his Son to save man from it, thinks you infatuated in neglecting this great salvation; and asks, in melting amazement, "Why will ye die?" The Savior who died to deliver from the wrath to come, thinks you ungrateful and irrational in keeping away from Him, and asks, "How often would I have gathered you under my wings?" Angels are amazed, and cry down from their thrones, "Who would not fear and glorify God?" for the great day of His wrath is coming. Well all these may!

So far, however, these hints and appeals create rather a whirl of thought and feeling, than give any definite character or direction to either. Indeed, if you would think to any purpose on this subject, you must think for yourself; and, like the high priest, when he entered the Holy of Holies, go "alone" within the veil. And this, though solemn, should not be difficult: for the invisible will soon be all as visible to you as it is eternal. Your soul must soon pass within the veil. It is not, it cannot, therefore, be impossible to enter in thought now. Your soul has all the powers now which it will have then. Then, indeed, its powers will be more powerful, and its emotions more prompt; but still it will be a reflecting spirit, a feeling spirit, a realizing spirit, amongst the realities of eternity. These will all be new to it, of course; but it will not have one new faculty of discernment or taste.

Eternity will burst upon the faculties you possess, and affect your spirit according to the moral state of your spirit. Then all the new scenes will act upon your old powers of mind and conscience. You will not be quite another being when you enter the judgment. You will be substantially, when you pass the boundary, whatever you are, intellectually and morally, when you touch the boundary between time and eternity. The transition will not transform an element nor an atom of your character. It will bring out all that is within you; but it will implant no new mental power or moral taste. It will complete and confirm your good or evil; but it will not alter your principles. You will be and do, think and feel, amidst the realities of eternity, exactly as you are affected by the revelations of them; and be as much yourself after death as before it.

It is, therefore, possible to tell, and therefore proper to try, how your spirit is likely to feel in the coming presence of the Lord. It can only feel in one of two ways; as a saved or as lost; and the natural emotions of either state are too strong to be doubtful or "hard to be understood." They reveal what they will be, the moment we suppose ourselves lost or saved. They break out at once in their true character.

Did you ever allow yourself to suppose the worst? I mean for the sole purpose of escaping it. It is, I know, too painful to dwell on long. Indeed, the spirit requires dragging, in order to bring it to the brink of hell; and chaining, in order to keep it there, until it is willing to "flee from the wrath to come." It is soon willing to get away from the vision of that wrath, and to forget the revelation of it. One look into the bottomless pit, however, makes the soul cry out. But the glance which extorts this shriek, does not endear Him who "delivereth from the wrath to come." The soul can rush away from the sight of it, without fleeing to Christ for refuge. Most souls, alas, flee to bustle or amusement, to forget all they saw and felt whilst looking at uncovered destruction. You have done so again and again. Even now, you are not willing to be drawn into a position which would compel you to realize the wrath to come.

You could ask—is it necessary to do so in order to be religious? You are inclined, perhaps, to argue, that working on your fears is not winning your heart. Well; I am quite ready to grant this. Love, not fear, is the principle of all true piety. But—if you do not love God or the Savior, holiness or devotion —you have cause for fear, and need for having your fears wrought upon. Besides, (for it is useless to conceal the fact), you have other fears, and dislikes too, than the direct terrors of this subject. You see, and dislike the sight, that you could not keep your eye on hell, and keep out of your closet so much. You are eagle-eyed in discerning how the fear of wrath would involve more devotion and self-denial than you think pleasant or convenient.

It is not, therefore, either your horror or hatred of hell that is the chief cause of your aversion to this subject. You are quite as much influenced by your dislike to certain duties which arise out of it, and by your distaste for that frame of spirit which the pursuit of heaven implies and enforces. In a word, you know very well, that were you in love with the way of salvation and holiness, you would have nothing to fear from any contemplation of the wrath to come. You fear to look at it, because you hate some of the things involved in fleeing from it. You know this to be true. You can neither deny nor palliate it. You dislike to think freely upon this point, because you dislike to act as it enjoins. Now, there are only two ways of overcoming this reluctance. Heaven must charm it away, or hell check it. The love of eternal happiness, or the dread of final misery, must bring it down. It will not go away, nor give way of itself. And, although grace alone can subdue it, and that only at the cross, neither grace nor the cross will act effectually upon it, apart from eternal things. Both originated and still reign for eternity; and, therefore, both work by eternity, and wield alternately around the soul its glories and terrors, to subdue the soul. If, therefore, all that you know or hope of heaven does not win you to faith and holiness by free choice, it is your duty, yea, your interest, to let the revelation of hell try all its power to disarm your prejudices against duty and devotion. That revelation of the wrath to come has both more power, and another kind of power, than you imagine. Its power to terrify is not its chief power. It can teach—melt—win—as well as awe and alarm.

Try, you will be more than agitated; you will be both instructed and stimulated, by allowing yourself to realize your natural and inevitable emotion, on the supposition of your spirit awakening amongst the lost. What! Can you not bear the thought? And yet—you risk the reality. Strange, sad infatuation! Afraid to think of hell, and yet not afraid to be afar off from the only refuge from it! Not safe, and yet set against taking such a look of your danger as would lead to safety. Come; this must not be. Do not yield to this temper. You must awake amongst the lost in reality, unless you allow yourself to look at them, until you love the way of escaping from their doom and company. It is only for this purpose that I entangle your spirit amongst the scenes and sensations of their spirits. I am "a man of like passions" with yourself. It is as unnatural and awful to me as it can be to you—to contemplate hell, marking my own emotions, and imagine cursing my infatuated folly for neglecting the great salvation: but this exercise must be done. There will be the old miser and the young spendthrift; the worldly and the wanton; the prayer-less and the creedless; the hypocrite and the formalist; the skeptic and the speculator; the intemperate and the intriguing; the mere philosopher and the merely sentimental. What else could be the effect of living even as the best of them did? There might have been no eternity, no salvation, no God, for any thing that the generality cared about religion. It was the last and the least thing in their estimation. Unless, therefore, it were a lie, nothing can be more true than that it flashes out with confounding majesty the moment they see it in the light of eternity.

Look at them again. In vain you try to palliate any man's neglect of salvation by the claims of his business, or the cares of his lot, or the strength of his passions. This nonsense may be talked at the gates of the market or the mansion, but not at the gates of hell. There—the soul alone appears valuable; salvation alone worthy of its love; piety alone seems common sense. You cannot doubt this, whilst you judge there. That place was not "prepared" for men, it was "prepared for the devil and his angels." And if they deserved it for one act of open rebellion against God, what else or less do men deserve, who lived a life of rebellion and neglect? Besides, what else are they fit for, who cared nothing about God; thought nothing about the Savior; and minded not the things of the Spirit? Not for heaven; for the Lamb is the glory of it, and they neglected him entirely: salvation is the theme of it, and they shut their eyes to the value and the necessity of its blessings; holiness is the beauty and the basis of heaven, and they hated it. Thus they lived and died, alienated and averse to all that constitutes the bliss of heaven, and made themselves fit only for hell.

You do not see this as I see it—and, what is worse, not as God shows it—if you can retire from the awful sight without trembling for yourself. The pleasures which betrayed the lost, tempt you; the gains which ensnared them, tempt you; the follies which infatuated them, tempt you; the sins which ruined them, tempt you; and you must sink as they will sink, if you act as they did. They will be left to the consequences of their foolish and criminal choice.

You now want to get away from this painful scene; and you shall. I have no wish to detain you at this scene of observation. If you have been long enough there in idea to be determined never to come there in reality, my purpose is answered, and your spirit is prepared to look in at the gates of heaven; for I want you to realize them before you reach them, and to anticipate the glory you desire.

How readily the spirit springs up from the gates of hell to the gates of heaven! This, however, is no proof of heavenly-mindedness. It is a proof that our spirits are capable of immortal happiness, and that, in some sense, they long for a glorious immortality, when a gloomy one has been vividly before them. But the real question is, what relish have our spirits for the heaven of the Bible, as the throne of God and the Lamb, and as the seat of holiness? We may love, indeed we cannot dislike, an eternity of joy and peace. An atheist could not hate that, nor a profligate despise it. God has taken care that no man can think lightly of the glory He has prepared for them that love Him, by making it too great and good to be unattractive. He has, however, made it all as holy as it is beautiful; and thus thrown us upon holy principles, as well as upon lofty prospects of happiness. We must love Him if we would live with him. We must be like Him if would see Him as he is. We must serve Him here if we would enjoy Him there. This, even all this, however, should not appear any hardship to you. It is both the bliss and glory of heaven. By pursuing this, you will reach the gates of the New Jerusalem; and there imperfection will fall off from your spirit, and you will enter into the city, to go no more out.

My aim, in this essay, has not been to realize for you; but to place you in positions where you may imagine and judge for yourself. Besides, I have been excluded from doing more by the essays which I addressed to the thoughtful, in my little work on "Eternity Realized."

6

Of Manly Realizations of Glory in the Church

Many who see much glory in Christ, seem utterly blind to the glory of the church of Christ. The advantage and honor, as well as the necessity of belonging to Him, they admit and feel; but they attach very little importance to union with His church, except for sacramental purposes. Many would not give "themselves to the church" at all, if they could reconcile the neglect of the sacrament with the duty of giving themselves fully "unto the Lord." Could they get over the point and pathos of His dying command, or obey that command out of the church, they would be quite content to have neither a name nor a place amongst the "living in Jerusalem." They would even prefer to have none, if they could persuade themselves that they ran no risk in disobeying the last injunction of the Savior. Thus they see neither sin nor danger in not giving themselves unto the church; feel neither loss nor shame for not belonging to it; but just so far as the neglect of the sacrament involves something of both.

If you think or feel so, you have never studied this subject. You may have glanced at it, and disputed about it; but you have not weighed it. No mind, capable of weighing it in the golden balances of the sanctuary, ever did so without feeling itself thrown, as it were, into a new world, with new ideas and emotions. The moment church fellowship is understood, it is appreciated. It is not fully understood by any man, who does not feel, through all his soul, that the act of joining the church on earth is next in sublimity and solemnity to the act of joining "the general assembly of the church of the first-born in heaven." Nothing is so like union with the church triumphant, as union with the church militant.

You do not understand either church, if this assertion seem doubtful or extravagant to you. And if you can smile at it, as official vaporing, or as ministerial complacency, pluming itself upon office, you do no credit to your own taste or discernment. For, what other society on earth bears any resemblance to the church in heaven? If the church on earth be not like it, all other assemblies are unlike it. The theatre, the ball-room, the banqueting-house, even the lecture room of science and literature, bear none of the image, and breathe none of the spirit of the general assembly. Thus, if the church has but little of the celestial aspect, the world has none of it. I do not forget that there are other religious societies, besides the churches of Christ. These, however, although "in the world," are not "of the world." Whatever likeness they bear to heaven, they derive from their connection with the churches. They, are, in fact, the children of the church of Christ: and thus living and lovely proofs that there is more glory in the church than superficial observers inquire or comprehend.

Your difficulty in discerning the real and full glory of the church arises, perhaps, from the state of the churches which fall immediately under your notice, and directly claim your company. You may see much poverty in one, and little piety in another. You may suspect, that in one communion you could have no friends, and in another too many acquaintances; in one place no distinction, and in another more distinction than would be either agreeable or convenient. Thus, between the extremes of no brotherhood on one side, and more brotherhood than you wish on the other side, you may have overlooked the true merits of church fellowship, hitherto; and, if this be the case, you cannot see them, until you cease to judge from the specimens before you. Indeed, you could not judge aright, even from the best specimen, if your own personal comfort or advantage be your chief object. The church exists for the world, and not chiefly for the solace or the safety of her individual members; except so far as they identify themselves with her grand object. Those who are long in the church without doing so, have as little enjoyment as those who keep out of it.

I am very anxious to interest you in this subject. It deserves your attention, however commonplace it may seem from these introductory hints: for all heaven is occupied and absorbed with the interests of the church on earth. She is the Father's family, the Son's inheritance, and the Spirit's temple. For her, the wheels of nature roll steadfastly, and the wheels of Providence wisely. To her, all the innumerable company of angels are ministering spirits; and all the events of time, purifying discipline or efficient help. In her, principalities and powers, although inhabiting heavenly places, learn "the manifold wisdom of God." Time cannot outlive the church, nor eternity displace or eclipse her in the divine favor. Her completion will be the signal for the end of time on earth, and for the jubilee of eternity throughout the universe. She is now "the salt of the earth," and "the light of the world;" and she will be forever the wonder of all worlds. She alone, of all the intelligent creation, is "the Bride, the Lamb's wife."

You forget all this, whilst you confine your attention to the little personal question—"What good would I get from joining any church in my neighborhood?" Indeed, you do not see these things, whilst you look either at a select handful, or at the promiscuous crowd of communicants. A church, in that light, may present few attractions to you, and make no impression on you, except so far as her attention to the sacrament reproves your neglect. You may even try in vain to associate the "glorious things spoken of Zion" with the little or the great hills of Zion around you, whilst you think only of those churches you can see. Any of them may seem, when tried by your standard of profit or pleasure, to promise but very little when they say, "Come with us, and we will do thee good." Perhaps, you have almost smiled at this invitation, and said to yourself, "What good could they do to me, beyond welcoming me to the sacrament, or visiting me if I were sick?" You ought to know better, than to argue thus. The poorest church of Christ can do you more real good than the wealthiest or the wisest society of philosophers. It can introduce you to the fellowship of the universal church of Christ; which neither the patent of kings nor the diploma of colleges could do. It can make you a fellow-citizen with the saints, and of the household of God; which you cannot make yourself, nor be made by any other society on earth. None but a church can give you a name and a place in the universal church of God.

And is it no "good" to be introduced, with fervent prayer and cordial welcomes, into "the sacramental host of God?" As you now stand, you are an "alien from the commonwealth" of his Israel, even if you be not a "stranger to the covenant of promise." Now, although this may not seem a great loss, nor a deep shame, so far as relates to the church which invites you, it is both in relation to the universal church. Not to be within her sacred pale, is awful and ignominious, even if it were not unsafe. Look at your position. It is repulsive, as well as perilous; shameful, as well as sinful; especially if you have given yourself to the Lord. In that case, your conduct is shocking. What! Rely on His blood, and withhold yourself from the church He purchased with his own blood? What! Own Him as "head," and refuse to be a member of that "body" of which He is head? What! Revere Him as the King of Zion, and yet keep out of Zion? Oh, had He cared as little for the church, as you have done, there would have been no salvation for you. Had He taken no more interest in her than you feel, she would have been unable to preserve or present to you the gospel of life and immortality. And were all who have given themselves to the Lord, to follow your example, there would soon be no church; and then, what would become of the world?

Again, I remind you, that it is not the claims of the church which directly appeals to you, that you have chiefly to consider. That individual church may labor under many disadvantages. It may be small, or poor, or despised by the world, or not very intelligent or harmonious in itself.

Thus it may have little attraction for you, and even expose you to some inconvenience. The question is, however, are there in it prayerful and holy men, confederated around the cross, and consecrated to the glory of God? If so, it is a church of Christ, warranted and qualified to introduce you to the fellowship of the universal church. It is, therefore, that "goodly fellowship" you are neglecting, whilst you stand aloof from the fellowship of its accredited agent, the church in your neighborhood.

You may not have intended nor seen this hitherto. You may have thought only of the local fellowship, and thus have overlooked the claims of the "goodly fellowship" to be had one day with prophets and apostles; of the noble army of martyrs; of the innumerable company of angels; of the just men made perfect in heaven.

It is, therefore, this vast, holy, and glorious communion that you have kept out of, whilst keeping out of the local fellowship of the saints. And, is this no loss?

Say not that it is rather an imaginary than a real loss. Is it an imaginary advantage to have relative and kindred spirits in heaven one day? You will not say so. You do not think so. You derive positive good and exquisite pleasure from the sweet consciousness that you will be related to the glorified. This is a powerful motive to follow their faith and patience. And is not brotherhood with "the whole family in heaven and on earth" a soothing consciousness, and a sublime motive? Would it not confirm your faith, and promote your holiness, and inspire your hopes to think that you were a joint heir with all the "great cloud of witnesses," and sure of the right hand of fellowship from all the hosts of heaven? Again, I say, it is from this communion of saints you stand apart, whilst you stand "without" the sacred pale of the Christian church. It will not mend this matter to say that you can realize the church in heaven, without giving yourself to the church on earth. If you can, that is an imaginary, not a real enjoyment. It is a mere sentimentalism. I mean that any pleasure you feel in thinking of their joys, is rather visionary than solid. It must be so whilst you have no strong sympathy with heaven's chief joy; that is, the prosperity and enlargement of the church of Christ.

Heaven's host rejoice chiefly in this, because this is His joy and glory; and thus you have not glorified Him. You, therefore, cannot identify yourself with the objects of their complacency; no, not even if angels have rejoiced over your repentance. If they have, it was in the fond hope that you would give yourself to the church, as well as unto the Lord; for, until you do so, the joy of angels over you is not perfect, and you have no part in their chief joy.

It should not, however, be necessary to "ascend into heaven," to bring down, from the church of the first-born, reasons for uniting with the church on earth. The earthly fellowship itself is "a goodly fellowship." It has, indeed, many defects, and some deformities; but it surpasses in beauty and power all the other social unions in the world. It wields a wider scepter than monarchs ever listed, and obtains an allegiance which crowns could not command.

The church is the heir of the world; and although much of it is not yet in her possession, the whole of it is destined to fall into her hands. The kingdoms of this world must all become, eventually, the kingdom of God and his Christ. The Alleluia of this consummation will as surely ring through the universe, as the prayer for it now rises to the throne. The will of God is sure to be done on earth as it is in heaven, whoever may doubt or oppose. Even now, all things give signs of the grand consummation. The winter of the moral world is past. The rain and hail of persecution are over and gone. The flowers of promise and proof appear on the earth. Even the time of the singing of the birds of the millennial paradise is come. But look at facts. They are more eloquent than figures, and more abundant too. There is not, at this moment, an idolatry under heaven, that is not trembling for its own existence, as well as tottering on its foundations. China itself feels that it is beleaguered, and can no longer wall out the church of God. Her oracles have thrown a spell upon the spirit of the empire, which, though not understood, fascinates and fixes its attention upon Britain and America, as the arbiters of its fate. Already the Bible is the schoolbook of India; and there, Buddhism despairs, and Hinduism is desperate. And yet, but a few years ago, China had no misgivings of heart, and no curiosity of hope or fear. Indian idolatry reckoned on British connection as its best safeguard from Mohammedan rivalry and Popish influence.

What has wrought this change, and made China and India feverish or feeble through all their moral frame? Not commercial companies, nor literary societies. Neither the factories of trade, nor the vice-regal thrones of power, gave the impulse to the native mind. The spirit of inquiry sprung from the labors of missionaries in the East. So it did in the South. Navigators discovered the islands of the Pacific, and commerce visited them; and both vitiated them. It was missionaries who civilized them, by Christianizing them. One vessel, the Duff, did more for Polynesia than all the ships which the Admiralty ever sent out, or all that Lloyds ever reported. No emblems, perhaps, illustrate so fully or so justly, the influence of the church upon the world, as those which Christ employed when he founded his church. Whilst his "little flock" sat at his feet on the mount, surrounded by the thousands of Israel, He pointed and appealed to his disciples, saying, "Ye are the salt of the earth, ye are the light of the world." This was language which Jews could not misunderstand. They heard Christ ascribe to his disciples a moral influence so mighty, that, like salt, it would preserve the earth from destruction, and like light fill it with glory. And this was no empty boast, nor extravagant compliment whatever it may have appeared at the time, to either His friends or enemies. Neither, perhaps, believed it at the time; but many years did not elapse before these bold words were proved to be "the words of truth and soberness." From the day of Pentecost, until the expulsion of the apostles from Jerusalem, Jerusalem saw, from the illumination of thousands of her own children, how the church of Christ would become the light of the world. It eclipsed, for a time, all the luminaries of the temple. It might have been "the cloud of glory" returned again to the mercy-seat, and absorbing all attention to itself; so completely did the new church outshine the old temple in gifts and graces. Multitudes, even of the priests as well as the people, believed. "A great company of priests were obedient to the faith." Acts 6:7.

Thus it was soon shown how the church was to be the light of the world: for, even in Jerusalem, the combined power of the altar and the throne could not extinguish nor eclipse her radiance. And that she was, emphatically, the salt of the earth, was signally proved on the same spot. The moment that the Christian church was withdrawn from Jerusalem, the city fell, "and great was the fall thereof." Whilst the Christians remained in it they were the salt of it. The Roman eagles could not tear the prey until the Christian doves flew to the mountains. Whilst they remained, their presence was a preserving salt to "the carcass" of the city and the nation.

Now, the real church of Christ has always been the salt of the earth and the light of the world. She has never so "lost her savor" as not to be both the preserving and purifying salt of the earth; nor ever lost her golden candlestick, as not to be the only true light of the world. Look well at this matter. I want you to see, with your own eyes, the conservative and sanctifying agency, which is the strength and hope of the world. Sciolists, and men who have not time to think, mystify this subject by "great swelling words" about patriotism, philosophy, commerce, the march of intellect, and the progress of society: as if these things explained, or had produced, or now upheld the present state of the world. These things themselves require to be accounted for. They have been, and are, the causes of much good; but the question is, what caused them? They are only the effects of superior causes. Neither their origin nor their efficiency is from themselves. All that is good or wise in national principles and character, has been taught, or sublimated, or sustained by the Christian church. She was the salt that preserved whatever was noble, humane, or enterprising in the nations she Christianized; and the light that led them on to whatever moral grandeur they may have reached. Without her, Britain and America could have done nothing of what is greatest and best in their character; just as, without Christ, her head, she could have done nothing for them or for the world. But, how few think of this!

How many, when this assertion is made, would say in the spirit of Nicodemus, "How can these things be?'" They are so accustomed to look at good kings, or wise cabinets, or wholesome laws, or glorious revolutions, as the real causes of national improvement, that they rarely notice the influence of the church. So little do the generality understand her character or place, that they would ask with a sneer, "What church is either the salt of the earth or the light of the world?" Having started this question, they would follow it up by affirming, that the Popish church has retarded the progress of society; that the Protestant establishments have not taken the lead in the march of civil or religious liberty; that the Voluntary churches are too poor or too much divided to put forth any great influence upon the world or the nation. When they have said all this, they imagine that the matter is settled, and turn with complacency to the politics, the literature, and the commercial spirit of the age, as the grand agencies and elements of the moral world. This is sheer trifling with both facts and principles!

The real and only church of Christ in the nation is the whole body of spiritual Christians. His British church is, and ever has been "the faithful in the land." And they are and they have been both its salt and its lights. But for them, the word of God would never have been translated into our own tongue, nor diffused throughout the nation. But for them, the worship of God would not have found sanctuaries, nor collected assemblies. It was the place which truth and devotion held in their hearts, that won for truth and devotion whatever place they have in the land. Had they loved the Bible or the sanctuary less, the Bible would not have given law to legislation, nor the sanctuary order to society. But they "held forth the word of life" so openly and steadfastly, so solemnly and devoutly, that kings were compelled to do it homage upon their thrones, and statesmen to adjust their policy to its principles.

A signal and sublime illustration of this has just occurred in the abolition of slavery. It will explain what I mean, and be itself best explained by the principle now before us. The commemorative medal of emancipation bears this motto, "This is the Lord's doing, and it is marvelous in our eyes." What less could any one say, who knows the history of either slavery or emancipation? No wonder if the champions of abolition should thus lay all the glory of the achievement at the feet of God and the Lamb. In vain would they try to find an explanation of the event in the spirit of a Reformed Parliament, or in the zeal of any Voluntary or State church. No denomination of Christians, as a denomination, did or attempted any thing that can account for such a consummation. Even missionary societies, as such, must join issue with the Anti-slavery Society, and exclaim, "This is the Lord's doing: it is marvelous in our eyes ," for, as societies, they all imposed silence upon their missionaries and schoolmasters, on the subject of slavery; and some of them did any thing, for years, but weaken the hands of slaveholders. Slavery never would have fallen before the ark of any society or church, which has a human name on the earth! It fell before the ark of the church of Christ, when its tabernacles were set on fire. The Society of Friends had much to do with emancipation, as a question of equity and humanity at home; but with the moral and spiritual preparation of the slave-mind for freedom, they had nothing to do. That was all "the Lord's doing." Their pity did not preach the gospel to slaves, nor their zeal plant education in the colonies. The Methodists also had much to do with the preparation of the slave-mind for freedom: nobody did more or better in paving the way of the Lord abroad; but, until their chapels were demolished, and their missionaries imprisoned, they had nothing to do with the progress of public opinion at home, on the abstract questions of right and policy. Even the Baptists threw no great weight into the scale at home, until oppression extorted their testimony. Like the Methodists, they bent all their energy on saving souls from the chains of darkness, and rather watched than urged on the progress of public opinion against colonial chains. Even the noble rally of the London Missionary Society around their "faithful martyr," Smith, bore far more upon the question of religious liberty than against African slavery. It asserted the rights of missionaries, and thus enabled them to maintain their post; but it left the rights of slaves to freedom undefended and undefined, except by implication. In like manner, the Churches of England and Scotland, as churches, had very little hand in the event. Both furnished some of the best champions of the holy war against slavery.

The first and best, Wilberforce, was a churchman. Thus all the British churches can honorably claim some place and part in the grand consummation; but none of them may wear, because none of them won, its laurels. It is "the Lord's doing." The Lord, however, does every thing of the kind by the instrumentality of His church. She was the salt by which He preserved British humanity from decay, and African passions from desperation. She was the light by which He led on British philanthropy to compensation, and African patience to prudence. Her devotional voice at the throne of God raised the public voice which roused the senate, and swayed the British throne. God, in answer to her prayers, and in blessing on her evangelizing enterprises, turned the hearts of men, like rivers of waters, into the channels of equity; and that spring-tide of national spirit carried every thing before it. The king could not hesitate, nor the legislature halt, until they sunk slavery like lead in the mighty waters, to rise no more forever.

Look more closely and deeply into this matter. This splendid event is only a specimen of the way in which God works. I mean, that there is nothing in it but an illustrious exemplification of the revealed fact, that His kingdom, or church, is the leaven by which He leavens the mass of society, whenever any great and good principle acquires the ascendency. It is the force of that principle, burning like "holy fire" at the heart of spiritual men, that inflames the men who desire to be spiritual; and through them warms into momentary vitality the half-hearted in religion; and, through the temporary spasm of their zeal, forces formalists into action, and hypocrites into assent; and thus neither neutrals nor despisers can resist. The impulse is thus propagated, though with diminished strength, from circle to circle, until it sway the community: but it came, like the circles in a lake, from the point where the moving cause cleft the surface, and sunk to the bottom.

It is, therefore, only the sober fact, that the eloquence of the senate, and the liberality of parliament, and the zeal of the press, and the spirit of the age, were merely the fermentation of the leaven which God first infused, and then rendered efficient. The men who first espoused and advocated African freedom were not candidates seeking popularity, nor senatorial patriots seeking the glory of their country. It was not a political question, nor a case of mere humanity. It was born in the hearts of spiritual men; cradled in the closet of secret devotion; and consecrated at the altar of public worship. It was taken up for God, in the fear of God, and with an express view to the glory of God and the Lamb. As might be expected, therefore, it won for a time only those who do and endure as seeing Him who is invisible. Philosophers did not think, nor senates speak for it, until the wrestling Jacobs of the land had filed so many petitions for it before the eternal throne, that they could not be silent when senators were chosen, nor when philosophers wrote. Then, but not until then, African freedom began to be a popular theme amongst political and worldly men. Thus, the original impulse came from heaven to the church, and through her was transmitted to the world. Real Christians moved nominal Christians; and they moved the senate and the press; and they moved society. Go up, therefore to the fountainhead of the influence which emancipated Africa, and you find it issuing like the river of life, from the throne of God and the Lamb. Wilberforce, and a few of his illustrious compeers, engraved the names of the African tribes upon their breastplates, and never appeared before God in Zion, or the closet, without interceding for them; nor before man, without stating their case.

The prayerful of the land saw this solemn and resolute intercession, and joined it fervently, though gradually. The pulpit took it up openly, and the vestry breathed it, and the family altar whispered it, and the closet echoed its unutterable groaning. Thus, the whole church of God bound the cause of Africa to their hearts. She found herself "bound in spirit," whilst colonial bondage continued; and "being in an agony she prayed more earnestly." And her effectual fervent prayer availed much.

Its importunate "Amen" shook the golden censer in the hand of the great High Priest before the throne; and when that censer was filled with "the prayers of all saints," He waved it once before the throne, and immediately voices were heard in heaven, and saying, "British slavery is fallen—is fallen to rise no more forever!"

Now, it fell, that the kingdom of God might rise. Its fall is merely one of those overturnings which make way for His coming, "Whose right it is to reign." The great work of the church, therefore, only begins where emancipation ends. The nation may pause now in its enterprise, or employ itself in immortalizing an unparalleled abolition, by medals and monuments of fame; but the church must neither pause nor play. She must go in and possess the land which the Lord her God hath given her. To her the political victory is only the signal for spiritual warfare. The abolition is merely the means of an infinitely nobler end— "the glorious liberty of the children of God!" Until this complete and crown the column of civil freedom, it is no pillar in the temple of God, and nothing on the scale of eternity. Until the Son make Africans free, they are not "free indeed." This digression is longer than I intended. It will, however, associate the principle of the essay with an event which is imperishably enshrined in your memory.

And now, observe how the history of the primitive church illustrates and confirms the principle. I want you to revere the church of God somewhat as you venerate the word of God. You would be ashamed of yourself, if you gave the Bible no place among your books, or an inferior place. You have reason to be so, whilst you are not identified with that church which Christ is not ashamed to plead for and employ. "The first works" of the first Christian churches bore no small resemblance to the finished works of creation. Both were "very good." Then, the church, like the sun, was the light of the world: like the sea, she flowed into all the channels of the earth, to cover them with the knowledge of the Lord: like the tree of life, she yielded her sanative leaves, for the healing of the nations, as freely as her ripe fruits for the nourishment of her children. Her works of faith embraced the spread of the truth she believed, as well as the personal character and spirit which should ever adorn its doctrines; and her labor of love aimed at the good of all men, as well as of the household of faith.

Whilst the Christian church was thus "fair as the sun," she was "terrible as an army with banners," to all temples and thrones where "glory to God and goodwill to men," were unknown or contemned principles. The Sanhedrim trembled at her holy aspect; it was at once so calm and heroic. The high priests of Jupiter and Baal recognized, in the moral and miraculous powers of the church, levers that would turn the world upside down, if plied in the same spirit as they had been planted on the vantage ground of Calvary. Philosophers and statesmen doubted very much whether "this work would come to naught." Even the Cesars suspected the stability of the imperial throne, and girt the purple more closely around them to conceal their fears. This involuntary homage of fear, thus universally paid to the church of Christ, by Judaism and heathenism, by philosophy and policy, must have been wrung from them by the evangelizing spirit of the church. Nothing but her avowed designs upon the whole world could have awakened such jealousy in all "high places;" for it began whilst her numbers were too few to be formidable, and whilst her resources could not exempt even her apostles from labor or poverty. The temples and thrones of that time, however much they may have hated the purity of faith or practice in the infant churches, could not have feared these churches, but for their public exhibition of the commission of Christ, to "preach the gospel to every creature."

That commission, however, as then held, and hallowed, and avowed by all Christians, was sufficient cause for political and ecclesiastical alarm, to all Jewish and heathen powers: for no man, prophet nor impostor, had ever dared to challenge the subjection of the whole world to "one faith." No handful of men, without money or influence, had ever set the world at defiance, or publicly pledged themselves to conquer it without carnal weapons. This was a "new thing on the earth;" and the rulers of the earth recognized its peculiarity at once. It had none of the forms of force or fraud, and nothing of the spirit of any sect or system, with which policy and power had ever grappled. Christianity was confident exactly in proportion to its apparent weakness, and its votaries waxed only more resolute as they were singled out for victims. The martyrdom of an apostle or an evangelist, instead of intimidating the adherents of the churches, rallied them, and determined undecided attendants to be baptized. Every champion that fell, fell like a grain of corn into the earth to produce much fruit.

What could senates or synagogues, priests or philosophers, make of all this? It was "not the manner of men;" and, accordingly, it baffled the sagacity of the master-spirits of the age. They had no rules nor experience which could fathom it. It defied their arms by meekness, and their arts by simplicity.

This was not, however, the only singularity of the primitive churches. They reposed all their hopes of success and safety upon the arm of God. "If God be for us who can be against us?" was a question which silenced all their own fears; and, as they never looked to any other quarter for support, and to Him only by prayer, it also staggered their enemies. They could give no answer to it. It was a question which defied their gods as well as themselves and thus forced upon them the idea of a God who despised all the divinities of Olympus and the Empyrean. And them, they could not shut their eyes to the fact, that, whoever He was, his worshippers evinced a confidence in Him which was unlike all popular faith, and unallied with any of the ordinary methods of propitiating the divine favor. It was not a confidence acquired nor sustained by attempts to appease His anger with costly sacrifices, or to win His aid by splendid temples. It gathered no strength from rich altars, nor from rigid penances. It simply leaned on the cross, and looked to the mercy-seat, by prayer alone. And, by that, it bore an aspect and breathed a spirit which were never seen around the altars of Greece or Rome, even when they flushed the heavens with the blaze of national holocausts. And then, all this holy confidence had respect chiefly to the spread of the gospel. It was not cherished by the first believers, for the mere sake of their own personal comfort or composure. They cultivated faith in God, in order that they might do the work, as well as suffer the will of God on earth. The apostolic churches felt themselves pledged, both by the letter and the spirit of the apostolic commission, to take care that the word of the Lord should "sound out" from them: that they should "hold forth the word of life," and thus be fellow-helpers to the truth.

They also lived, avowedly and habitually, for eternity. In its solemn lights and shadows, they looked upon the perishing world at large, and upon the souls of their immediate neighbors. They so realized the judgment-seat of Christ, that they kept, as it were, His commission forever lying upon it, as one of "the books which will be opened," when the saved are confronted with the lost. Thus they seem to have read it with much of the same spirit as they expected to hear it, when the Judge should try their stewardship "of the manifold grace of God," by what they had done to make that grace "appear unto all men." Accordingly, they exerted themselves to be and do all for the world, which the hope or fear of meeting the world at the bar of God inspired.

It is, I am aware, as easy to pay sweeping compliments to primitive times, as to advance sweeping charges against modern times. I do not, however, forget that all this is not true of all the first Christians individually, nor equally true of all the first churches. There were tares amongst the wheat even then. This, however, only renders "the first works" of the churches which did work, the more amazing. The wonder increases, by the decrease of numbers, which is thus forced upon our notice, when we take into account the faults and factions recorded and reproved in the Epistles to the churches. This, like the thinning of Gideon's army, only makes the vigor and victories of the working churches the more signal and surprising. The historical details of what they did and attempted, "as good stewards of the manifold grace of God," are not necessary here, in order to justify the general view now given of their character and labors. The well-known actual results of primitive zeal and fidelity, prove how much they must have done and attempted for the conversion of the world. The world was soon turned "upside down;" and they did it. Judaism did not fall in Palestine by its own weight, nor by the Roman arms, until Christians had sapped its foundations. Platonism was not displaced in Greece, nor Epicureanism in Rome, without Christian effort and prayer. The olive of Minerva did not wither upon the Hymettus, nor the laurel of Mars upon mount Aventine, from age; but from successive scathings of holy fire, scattered by holy men. The temples of Jupiter were not forsaken, without being summoned and assailed; nor the altars of Venus overthrown without a struggle. The heathenism of the eastern and western empire faded and fell, before the brightness of the eastern and western churches. Their doves gave battle to all the eagles of Baal and Jupiter; and although the doves bled, they so multiplied, that the eagles were blinded and worn out.

Christianity thus fought every step of her way, with the sword of the Spirit, from an upper room in Jerusalem, into the seats of Philosophy, and the palace of Cesar. Alone she did it! Wherever her children laid her "sure foundation stone" of hope and holiness, they had to roll it up mountains of peril, and through valleys of privation, with their own hands, and at their own expense. God was, indeed, with them; but they also were with Him. They wrought for him, whilst He wrought by them. All "the increase," He gave by His Spirit, was given to the planting and watering of his word in the field of the world. All that increase was, however, emphatically, not by their might nor by their power, but "by the Spirit of the Lord;" for whatever might or power they had, He both created and sustained it.

It was all the fruit of the Spirit. Their will and power to work for God, as well as the success of their labor, came down from the same source. This spread of the gospel during the first and second centuries, was so rapid, irresistible, and extensive, that it cannot be at all accounted for by any human means or principles. Nothing explains it rationally, but the work of the Holy Spirit, and the workings of a special providence cooperating effectually with efficient Christian means and efforts.

But this process, however supernatural, explains it all as naturally as sun and rain account for seedtime and harvest. It is not, therefore, without cause, that theologians charge infidels with absurdity as well as impiety, for attempting to refer the spread of the gospel to human means and local circumstances. Gibbon merges the historian in the theorist; Hume, the philosopher, in the fanatic; and Voltaire and Volney, the man in the monkey—when they attempt this. They could not have evinced more arrant folly or arrogant effrontery, had they set themselves to prove that seed and soil, if well managed, can produce harvest without sun and rain.

It is equally instructive and delightful to trace the early triumphs of Christianity throughout the Roman Empire. They at once evince the truth of the gospel, and unveil the secrets of its success, and thus send a glowing impulse to the heart, in favor of fellowship with "the communion of saints." Who would be an "alien" from that commonwealth of Israel, which God has so long sustained and signally honored? "Come in, thou blessed of the Lord; why standest thou without!"

7

On Manly Realizations of Christ in the Bible

Were you ever struck with John's sublime summary of Revelation, when he says of Christ, "In Him was life; and the life was the light of men?" If not, the study of it will make the diamond of truth blaze with new splendor.

When you consider that God is invisible, and that eternal things are unseen—is it not astonishing that we know so much of both? Both, indeed, surpass all comprehension; but neither infinity, nor their invisibility, prevents us from knowing enough for our satisfaction. We have, in regard to God and eternity, as much light as we can use; and need be at no loss what to think of Him or it. Accordingly, we are not, in general; but have, upon the whole, such ideas of God as confirm our sense of obligation, and such views of the future state as impress our minds, whenever we reflect seriously.

Our knowledge of these unseen objects, however limited and superficial, compared to what it might be, yet, compared with the dim and deformed notions of the heathen, is open vision; compared even with the clearest and loftiest discoveries of human philosophy, it is so; for the world even by wisdom knew not God. Infidel philosophers may boast of sitting at the feet of Plato and Socrates; but if Plato and Socrates were the men they are said to have been, and alive now, they would give their own palm to a well-educated child in a Sunday school. I mean, in matters of religion: for such ideas as, God is love—God is a Father—God is just, and yet a Savior—never dawned upon their mighty minds, as facts or conjectures. This, however, is the light in which God appears to us; in which we think and speak of Him. In some form or other, we are as familiar with the idea of His being a Father, as of His being a Judge.

Why is this; to what are we indebted for this superior knowledge of God and eternity? The light of men on these subjects is now perfect day, compared with the brightest periods of the light of nature. What created the difference? You are ready to say, the Bible. Revelation has unveiled the true character of God: life and immortality are brought to light by the gospel. All the true light in the world has shone from the oracles of God. True: but when you have said all this, you surely do not think that you have traced the light of men to its original source. All the natural light we enjoy is from the sun: but He is only the reservoir of it. Light itself was created before the sun, and sprang forth at the command of God. In like manner, the Bible is to divine light what the body of the sun is to natural light: not the original source of it, but that which contains and disperses it. The life is the light of men; and the Bible is full of light, because it is full of Christ—the Author of eternal life.

Perhaps, at first sight, this may seem a distinction without a difference; for unless you have been very much struck with the fact itself, you will hardly anticipate the use I am about to make of it, nor the exact point to which the distinction will lead. It is, however, an important one; and should I succeed in explaining it, the effect will be, not to change your views of the Bible, but to exalt them.

Now, observe: We are indebted to the Bible for all our light in matters of religion; to what, then, are we indebted for the Bible itself? All our light comes from it; from whence, then, came its own light? The Bible is our sun; but from what source was it filled with the light it diffuses: the common answer to such questions is, "The Bible is the word of God; we are indebted to Him for all it reveals." True: this answer is correct so far; but it does not go far enough. In this general form it leaves uncertain, indeed unseen, the motive which led God to reveal His will —the principle which guided that revelation—and the character too, in which God spoke. I ask, therefore, again, to what feeling or purpose of the Eternal Mind are we indebted for the word of God? In what capacity did He speak to the world? As a Sovereign, or as a Lawgiver, or as a Judge, or as a Father? If you say, "He has spoken something in each capacity," then I ask again, which capacity took the lead in revelation? Whether has He said most, as King or as Father? What predominates in His word—love or law? This matter should not be disposed of by merely saying that a revelation of the divine will was necessary for man as an accountable being, and therefore God gave him one: the question still returns, "Why did God give us His word, and in what character did He speak?"

Now, it is not a direct answer to this inquiry to say, that from a Being infinitely good, a revelation of some kind might naturally be expected. This is the ground usually taken in arguing with Deists. Accordingly, so far as I can recollect the character of the leading books written in defense of the Bible, the probability, propriety, and necessity, of a revelation from God to man, is the basis of all the reasoning. The defenders press Deists with such questions as the following: "Would it not be worthy of God to communicate some knowledge of Himself to his creatures? Is it likely that the Father of our spirits should leave them in ignorance, or to mere conjecture? If we are accountable and immortal, is it not reasonable to expect some information in regard to the grounds of our responsibility, and the nature of our prospects?" These are solemn and solid points, and both unanswered and unanswerable by any infidel who admits the being and beneficence of God. But while I admire such methods of accounting for the Bible to those who deny its divine origin, I object to the frequent use of them amongst those who receive the Bible as the word of God. They, at least, and especially those who believe with the heart, should be treated in another way than Deists; should be made and kept fully aware, not only of the general principles which secured a revelation to man, but also of the leading principle or cause which produced that revelation we have; for the circumstances which account for one of some kind, will not account for it. The Bible reveals the free gift of eternal life to sinners, through the death of the Son of God; and this is a matter so singular, a plan so sublime, a measure so far removed from both the letter and the spirit of natural religion, that no human reasonings are applicable to it. Our being accountable does not warrant the expectation of, much less establish a right to, such a gift. It may be only just that we should know something of the God with Whom we have to do; and only fair to have a bible of some kind; but such a bible as we have is infinitely beyond all that could be rationally expected as right or favor.

Hence the necessity of questioning and cross-questioning ourselves, until we are fully sensible of the real source from whence so much light has flowed into the Bible. Now John explains this: "The life was the light of men."

The gift of eternal life through Christ led to all that is said or shown in Scripture. To predict that gift, or to explain it, or to commend it, is the grand object of revelation, and the positive cause of it. The Bible is full of light, just because Christ is full of life: the light that is in it is the exhibition of the life that is in Him. Had there been no life in Christ for man, there would have been no light for man, but the light of nature. You begin now to perceive what I am aiming at, and, I hope, to perceive that the subject is likely to repay the attention it is sure to require. I cannot simplify it at once, but if you follow me, you will be familiar with it before we close.

Now, John sums up the contents of the Bible thus: "This is the record, that God hath given to us eternal life; and that life is in his Son." As if the apostle had said, "Scripture records nothing but what is, in some way, connected with the gift of eternal light." Men have light, just because they may have life. In this point of view the Bible assumes quite a new aspect, and comes before us, not only as the word of God, but also as "the word of life." Let us, therefore, review the successive

MANLY PIETY IN ITS REALIZATIONS

revelations given to man as light emanating from the eternal life which is in Christ.

Eternal life was forfeited by the fall. The loss of holiness involved the loss of heaven. Death temporal, spiritual, and eternal, came by sin, and must have continued, had not God provided a Savior, who died that we might live. This the Son of God did, and thus became a quickening, or a life-giving, Spirit; the right of bestowing eternal life being the reward of his own death. This glorious event did not, however, actually take place until the fullness of time: an interval of four thousand years elapsed before Christ appeared, declaring, "The bread that I will give is My flesh, which I will give for the life of the world." But during that long interval, frequent intimations of His life-giving death were received from heaven, and these were the light of man in every age, brightening, as it shone, into the perfect day. The promise of the gift of eternal life through Christ was the light of our first parents, and of the first families of mankind. The religious knowledge which cheered and encouraged them in a world of sin and death, was not the lingering twilight of the sun which set in Eden, but the predicted rising of the Sun of Righteousness; was not what the first Adam recollected of God and glory, but the revelation of what the last Adam should do. Their light shone, not from the wrecks of the Eden economy, nor from a new system of laws, but from the promise of eternal life by Christ.

Now, this is both a more distinct and scriptural idea than merely saying that God revealed His character and will to the world again, after the knowledge of them was lost by sin. This is true; but for any thing that appears upon the surface of the statement, the new revelation might be nothing more than knowledge, nothing better than the reassertion of the divine authority and government; whereas, the real fact is, that all the knowledge was the knowledge of salvation; all the light the promise of eternal life.

Whatever laws, ordinances, or councils, were given to the first families of mankind, were grounded upon the promise of a Savior, sprung out of it, and led to it. As the cherubim and flaming sword upon the gate of Eden kept the way to the tree of life, so all the new commands and appointments of God were measures for manifesting His gracious purpose of sending His Son to be the life of the world. This gives quite a new character to the early revelations of divine things. While we think of them merely as knowledge, and compare them with our own light, they seem too few and feeble to have had much interest or effect; but in supposing this, we forget that they all concerned eternal life through the death of Christ; an object so dazzling in itself, that it could not be presented so dimly as to be uninteresting. In any shape or degree of manifestation, it must have been a burning and shining light, because it was the only light. If God did not, therefore, speak so plainly nor so fully then, as he has done since, what He did say was all on one subject, and that subject the chief thing which belongs to the eternal peace of man: salvation was the matter, whatever was the manner of revelation.

You see I am anxious to fix your attention on this fact; but not merely to prevent you from thinking too lightly of the first oracles of God, but to keep you from the common way of thinking about the Bible in general. We are apt to think of the successive revelations it contains, as a series of instances of God's laying down law to his creatures; of God's asserting his authority over man; of God fixing the absolute rule of faith and practice; of God denouncing sin, and enforcing duty. Now, this is neither a full nor a fair view of the matter; and, accordingly, it has no winning or sweet influence upon the mind. With the Bible before us, in this light, we are both capable and inclined to wish that its laws were less numerous and strict; its sanctions less formidable and solemn, its doctrines less mysterious and absolute. This is the natural effect of forgetting, or not understanding, the apostolic principle.

All the lights of the Bible shine from the eternal life that is in Christ. Every thing written for our instruction has for its chief and first object, to endear God to us as the God of salvation. If, therefore, He denounce sin, it is because He is intent on saving us from it; if He demand obedience, it is because He will give grace to produce it; and if the doctrines of His word are absolute, and admit of no rejection, it is because they are the power of God unto salvation. Life, spiritual life here, and eternal life hereafter, is the source and center of all we are bound to do or believe. This view of the matter will become more obvious and interesting as we proceed.

The covenants which ratified the promise of eternal life through Christ were the light of men in the patriarchal age. When the deafening roar of the deluge was silenced by the subsiding of the waters, God spoke again to man. His voice was heard on Mount Ararat, as it had been in Eden; and again the life was the light of man. Gospel, not law breathed in the covenant ratified with Noah. The word of God, to him, was not an exposure of the crimes which brought the flood upon the world; not even a warning against them; the flood itself was left to do all this by the sound of its many waters; and God, as usual confined Himself to publishing salvation.

The eternal purpose of sending his Son to be the life of the world, had been in nowise shaken by the ungodliness of the world; and that it might appear unshaken amidst the shattered frame of nature, no time was lost in making it dart forth new light upon man. Thus it did; and as the tree of life, that original emblem of the covenant of peace, had been engulfed by the deluge, the rainbow of the heavens was assumed as the symbol in its stead, and every law given to the family of Noah was a light shed upon the promise of a Savior.

In the same spirit the covenant was ratified with Abraham. The increased light of his period shone from the life treasured up in Christ. And this, as in the case of the first families of mankind, is the cause why so little was said to the patriarchs. Much was not necessary when all related to "the one thing needful," and, that being the gift of eternal life through Christ, it was hardly possible to state it so slightly as to leave it uninteresting. Accordingly, we never hear of any of the patriarchs complaining of what, compared with our own, we should call dim discoveries of the way of salvation. Abraham rejoiced to see the day of Christ afar off: in faith of it, Isaac submitted calmly to be laid on the altar. In a similar spirit Jacob waited for the salvation of God. All this is wonderful, upon the usual supposition of their knowing so little: but the wonder ceases the moment we understand that the life was the light of man in all ages. For, although the plan of salvation did not come before the patriarchs, enshrined in all the light of its fulfillment, neither did it come before them encumbered, as it now is, with the controversies of the world. The only point at issue, then, was, whether Jehovah or Baal was the true God: and those who believe Jehovah to be so, were left by others to the undisputed possession of all they knew or hoped of a Savior.

Thus the life being their light, very little of it was amply sufficient, in such a state of society as the patriarchs lived in. And this was the object and character of all their knowledge: if they were commanded to build altars and burn sacrifices, these pointed to the Lamb slain: if they were sent out as pilgrims to Canaan, Canaan was the type and pledge of that heaven, which is the seat and consummation of eternal life.

Here, again, I ask you to pause and observe how the revelations vouchsafed by God, were not assertions of his authority as God; not demonstrations of his being or will; but disclosures of the purposes of grace, proofs of His willingness to save, and exhibitions of the plan of salvation. All He said by His word, and all He did by his providence, bore upon this one point. Not a single ray of light shone from the Father of lights, but what led to Christ as the Author of eternal life. Even the light shed upon men by the Mosaic dispensation, shone from the purpose and promise of life through the death of Christ. Yes, under what Paul calls the ministration of death, "the life was the light of men." These two assertions are not in the least contradictory nor incompatible. Paul himself both makes them and reconciles them, in Gal. 3:17, that promise was the gift of eternal life through Christ, which, instead of being set aside by the law, was made sure by it. Accordingly, Paul argues, "who was that seed in whom the promise was to be fulfilled." Agreeably to this view of the matter, the law itself is expressly said to be a schoolmaster to bring men to Christ, and a witness in common with the prophets to the righteousness which is by faith in Christ. Romans 3:21, 22.

Thus the law itself witnessed in favor of the principle of justification without the law; and was, therefore, itself, light from the life treasured up in Christ. There is solid and harmonious sense in this view of the matter: whereas it is the mere jargon of a human system, to call the law a covenant of works, made with the Jews. They, indeed, considered it as such, and turned it against grace; but that abuse of it did not alter its own nature. The direct light which beamed from the law, not only showed the necessity of the promised Savior; but, from its connection with the covenant and the sacrifices, actually pointed to Him as the only refuge of the guilty. Distinguish, therefore, and understand: when the Scriptures contrast the law and the gospel, it is not the law as given by God in connection with the promise of eternal life; but the law as turned by men into the condition of life, or as taken up and adhered to in opposition unto or in partnership with Christ.

Against this the New Testament bends all the force of its reasoning and all the fire of its remonstrances, until the law of God almost seems the chief enemy of the gospel of God: but it requires only a moment's consideration to be convinced, that man makes it this enemy and not God. God never would have introduced and established a system subversive of the gospel, or at variance with the covenant of grace. It is absurd to imagine such a thing. Accordingly, the law, as He gave it, and keeps it, and intends it, is itself light from the gift of life; for, had not God purposed to bestow eternal life through His Son, He would never have given law to sinners; indeed, it would have been useless to do so: for, what could sinners have made of it? Absolutely nothing. But now, by the law, is the knowledge of sin: and as, without that knowledge, men neither know the value nor feel the need of a Savior, the law may well be considered as a light leading to Christ. Its heaviest curse and hardest rules, are, therefore, direct methods of endearing that Savior, who, that He might give life, died to satisfy both.

I have condensed into a small compass the pith of this vast subject; and though it amply deserves more illustration, I must leave it, by again asking you to observe, how, in the most terrific period of revelation, it was not in the mere character of a Sovereign, that God spoke: even while giving law in thunder upon Mount Sinai, "the life was still the light of men." God was only taking necessary and effectual measures for maintaining the knowledge, and explaining the nature, of His eternal purposes of grace and salvation. If I have succeeded in proving this to your satisfaction, it will now be almost needless to show how all the light diffused by prophecy originated from the life treasured up in Christ. This must be a self-evident proposition, when you remember that to Him all the prophets gave witness. I therefore pass it, and proceed to show how the settled purpose and plan of giving eternal life through the death of Christ, led to the giving of all the light which revelation has shed upon the world.

The plan of salvation is the manifold wisdom of God, and embodies in itself both all the love and all the glory of the Deity. Now if the defenders of revelation argue from the infinite perfection of God, that a Bible of some kind might be expected, and would be a gift worthy of such a Being, then I argue that such a Bible as ours was sure, since that Being had resolved to bestow eternal life through his Son; because such a resolution deserved to be made known. Nothing so glorious as salvation had ever emanated from God: nothing equally glorious ever can emanate from Him; because the death of His Son will never be repeated, whatever moral changes may take place in the universe during the lapses of eternity: for, now Christ ever liveth. Such being the real state of the case, it was not likely that God would conceal the purposes and plans of such grace: they had occupied the Eternal Mind so long and deeply, engaged the eternal sympathies and feelings so entirely, and were so intimately connected both with the glory and government of God, that He was as sure to reveal His generous purposes, as to form them. He owed it to Himself, to exhibit the magnificent results of His everlasting counsels and infinite love; and as His own happiness could not be increased by suppressing, nor diminished by disclosing, the knowledge of them, the very character of God secured to man light concerning that life He had decreed to give. Besides, no good end could have been answered, by hiding the purpose: indeed, the only effect of such a measure would have been the surprise of those who were taken to heaven without knowing why or how, or what it was: a state of mind equally unworthy of God, and unfit for glory. There will be enough of surprise as it is.

The plan of salvation required to be made known. It is no affectation when I preface this remark by declaring, that I know not what to say first; so many cogent reasons throng in, claiming precedence of each other, that I am at a loss which to choose. However, I cannot choose wrong. Well, the plan required to be made known; for otherwise it would not be executed. It embraced the ministering angels; and that involved the disclosure of it in heaven, that they might know what they had to do for the Savior and the heirs of salvation. It embraced the system of animal sacrifice for ages to illustrate its grand principle, that without shedding of blood there is no remission; and that could only be introduced by publicly assigning the reasons for such a measure. It embraced the incarnation of the Son of God; and that could only be accomplished honorably by being foretold openly, and the object of it explained clearly. It embraced the humiliation of the Son of God; and that could not be effected but by sending Him into the world. It embraced His sufferings and death; and those could not have been brought about so that men could have known them to be an atonement, without knowing beforehand how He was to suffer and die. Thus the historical parts of the plan of salvation involved the necessity of revelation: the life had to give light, in order to lead naturally to the death of Christ. But this is too general.

One chief part of eternal life is, we are assured, to know the only true God, and Jesus Christ whom He hath sent; and this secured a revelation of Their character as the means of knowing Them. Another chief ingredient of eternal life is holiness; and as true holiness is the holiness of the truth, or conformity to the will of God, this secured a revelation of His will. And heaven being the consummation of eternal life, and no purpose to be answered by concealing it from those who were to inherit it, the gospel of life naturally brought immortality to light. Since, then, all scriptural light has sprung from the gift of eternal life in Christ, how shameful and sinful is it to trifle with the light of the gospel. This is a crime of far greater magnitude and malignity than appears by saying, of the careless, they do not read their Bibles, nor reflect upon the word of God. This, would, indeed, be bad enough whatever the Bible contained. This is nothing, compared with their neglect. They are trifling, not so much with eternal law, as with eternal life; not so directly with divine authority, as with infinite love. You may imagine that they are only evading duties not convenient at present; only postponing things not agreeable. Deluded judges! They are pouring contempt upon the most glorious salvation which the united Godhead could devise; risking souls which all heaven rushed to save; trifling with eternal life.

What a horrid spectacle is a careless man in this point of view. The Father beseeching; the Son bleeding; the Spirit striving; and yet the sinner resisting, and smiling at the ease with which he can take the matter. Heaven open in all its glory; hell uncovered in all its gloom; and yet the sinner standing as unmoved as if he were an idiot! What shall I say? I could speak daggers to the unconcerned, if I could forget that I myself was once equally thoughtless. But I cannot forget the wormwood and gall of that state: my soul has them still in remembrance, and is humbled within me. Oh! View not the great salvation in a wrong light! It is your life; your eternal all is involved in it, and every act of neglect is an outrage upon boundless, beseeching, bleeding, dying love.

Have pity, have pity upon your own mortal soul. All heaven cares for it; and will you care nothing? By the mercies of the Lord, by the terrors of the Lord, I implore you to pause and weigh the matter. Since, them, all scriptural light has sprung from eternal life, with what lively attention and adoring wonder we ought to study the word of God! Integrating it merely as a lesson or lecture about religion, or even as the standard of truth and holiness, is a poor, tame, soulless feeling, when eternal life is the substance of the Bible. Why, revelation is mercy rolling back the curtains of the eternal throne, to unveil the God of love; is mercy moving forward that throne, to render the Lamb slain visible in the midst of it; is mercy disclosing the river of life, flowing full and free from it; is mercy pointing to crowns and mansions of glory; is mercy leading forward.

Eternity, glowing with the immortal splendor of all that God has done or will do, laden with the weight of glory, resounding with the alleluias of the universe, and teeming with the future wonders which through everlasting ages shall bless as they blaze, the general assembly of saints and angels.

May you awake to the grandeur and grace of the Bible! It is the telescope by which two eternities are rendered visible; each thronged with stars which shine to guide, to cheer, to exalt, and which will shine forever and ever! The past eternity, like the milky-way of the material heavens, is seen crowded with the redeeming purposes, and plans, and covenant of grace: the coming eternity, rich and radiant with the scenes and felicities of

8

Manly Realizations of Future Probabilities

Strong and prying as human curiosity is, it is somewhat cowardly too. It would hardly venture to break the seals of a book which really foretold all the events and vicissitudes of future life; unless it had some reason to hope that there was more good than evil contained in the predictions; and, even in that case, both the hand and heart would tremble not a little, lest the evil should be of that kind which we dread most. Accordingly, we are very curious only about the good which may happen to us. Any wish we feel to know the worst, is not strong enough to make the knowledge at all tempting to us, even if we could obtain it.

This was the real character of human curiosity about the future, even when oracles and omens, divination and astrology, were at the very height of their popularity. There was, indeed, then, a rage for prying into the book of fate, and for extorting the secrets of the stars and the grave, at any expense or peril. It was not, however, for the sake of knowing the worst, that these experiments were tried. A desperate king, or a daring usurper, when frenzied by the crisis of his affairs, courted the knowledge of the worst recklessly, because nothing could be worse than a crisis in his fortune. It was, therefore, no great hardihood to hazard the most fatal response of an oracle, when death or defeat was inevitable from the pressure of circumstances. And in regard to others, their passion for prying into secret things was the hope of finding them better than past or present things. No man ever wished to know how much evil awaited him, until his affairs were absolutely desperate.

The age of oracles and incantations is happily gone by forever; but curiosity about the future remains still. We are no longer superstitious; but we continue to be imaginative, and to allow both hope and fear to push forward their conjectures amongst the secrets of futurity. We look to the visions, and listen to the voices of our own wishes, quite as much as the ancient heathen did to their divinations; and are as much led by them too. For, who has not studied his own prospects in life, and laid his plans accordingly? Thus we are our own oracles now. Delphos and Dedona are in our hearts. We despise the witch of Endor; but we listen as attentively to the whispers of our own hopes, as Saul did to the necromantic visions. We conjecture as much as the ancients conjectured. This natural solicitude about our success in life may be turned to a good account, by wise management. We cannot shake it off altogether; but we may regulate it. It may even be indulged so as to prove very useful.

Now, in regard to future life, you have, of course, more hopes than fears. You hope the best in your own case. I mean, you take for granted that you will have more joy than sorrow in the world. You see no reason, and feel no inclination, to fear the worst. You are not unwilling to do well, in order to succeed well; and, therefore, hope that things will not turn out ill. Well: suppose the best. Take for granted, if you will, the success of your business—the permanency of your health—the weight of your public character—the worth of your private friends—and the completion of that "home, which plighted love endears."

Now, seat yourself at the fire side you thus wish for yourself. Place opposite to you, in light and loveliness, "the desire of your eyes." Look around upon a select library, and a still more select group of pictures, and out upon a sweet garden. Let your cabinet too, be rich in real, and the shelf by your easy chair piled with all the best periodicals. Let music also breathe its charms over the whole scene of this home. Call in, too, the occasional presence of your bosom-friend, and of your most intelligent associates. Look at the image of your happiness, as it is reflected in their enjoyment. Is not all this enough? You see, at a glance, how willingly you would go out to business in the morning, and how cheerfully you would go through it all the day, in order to keep up such a home. You feel, at your heart, how readily you would return at night to the quiet and refreshing joys of domestic life. Now, this is the utmost, the best, that can be realized: for I will not suppose, that you would reckon revelry or cards any addition to this pleasure. Its tranquility and rationality form its chief charm.

Would, then, this please you? Well, suppose it all your own, and your own for life, what is it all without piety? No prelude of heaven. There is music, but not that which eternity will prolong. There is reading, but not that which maketh wise unto salvation. There is taste, but not for objects or subjects which prepare for a death-bed. There is love, but not that love which is a pledge of reunion and fellowship in the mansions of immortality. Thus the fair body of happiness has no deathless spirit in it. It is altogether "of the earth, earthy." Could you be satisfied with such a home? Why, without piety, it could only embitter.

"But why should it be without piety?" you ask. Nay, it is for you to answer that question. What place or provision does your plan make for that piety which saves the soul, and makes meet for heaven? When building and beautifying this fabric of happiness, did you even think of founding it on "repentance towards God, and faith in our Lord Jesus Christ?" Did you even select the books for your anticipated library, with any express reference to becoming wise unto salvation? When you realized music, had it any reference to family worship? Did you propose to yourself, in furnishing your future home, that the table of your sitting-room should be a family altar for the morning and evening sacrifice; and that one chair in your study should be a sacred footstool, at which you would kneel before God in secret? When you laid out your garden in thought, did you at all intend to be found in its bower, or beneath its shady trees, like Nathanael "under the fig-tree;" or like Isaac in "the fields at eventide," musing and praying over eternal things? If not, look again at this "house made with hands;" it has no connection with that house "not made with hands, eternal in the heavens." It is everything that human hands can make it; but no divine hand is upon it, in blessing or guardianship. It even defies God, by excluding God: for the house that "is not for Him is against Him."

Perhaps you take for granted, that such a tabernacle as you anticipate and desire, would be sure to make room for religion. I, therefore, refer you at once to the tabernacles from which you model your own. How many of them echo "the voice of rejoicing and salvation?" In most of them, all the music is without praise; all the reading without prayer; and all the social intercourse, neither sanctified nor sweetened by any hope of glory. Their whole routine terminates upon this world. How, then, is it sure, that your house, would be an exception to the general run of such houses?

Having thus supposed the best, and seen that it is no security for piety, let us now suppose the worst, and see how you are prepared to meet it. I do not say, suspect the worst, such foreboding is forbidden. All I want is that you look at the instances around you, in which health has broken down; in which property has been lost; in which business is nothing but embarrassment; marriage, misery; and a sickly family, a source of perpetual and wasting anxiety. There are such scenes on your right hand and on your left, and those who suffer in them had as little expectation of such suffering as you can have. But, there they are. Out of it they cannot get. They must bear up, and struggle on, as they can. This may be your lot: for it is not always the effect of misconduct. There is ill health, where there have not been bad habits; and embarrassment, where there has not been imprudence in business; and family affliction, where domestic love is not wanting.

Now, place yourself in realizing thought, for a moment, in one of these scenes of care and privation. Think of dragging a frail body and an uneasy mind, day after day, to an unproductive and precarious business; of returning, night after night, to a charmless and cheerless home; of having no prospect of bettering your condition, and no great security against its becoming worse. Are you at all prepared for this, should this be prepared for you? It is prepared for many who now hope, as you do, for better things. It is now endured by many who, at your time of life, had as little reason to fear it as you can have. It is, therefore, not impossible in your case. Have you, then, any one principle of endurance or resignation that could stand the tear and wear of such trials? Have you any such hold upon the hope of eternal life, as would be likely to sustain you in a life of toil and trouble? Is the salvation of your soul so precious to you, that it invests even this sad prospect with reasons for faith and holiness? Or, do you feel that, in such a lot, you could not be pious? Perhaps, you feel something worse than this rising within you. Remember, however, that there are also those, who have to do and suffer all that I have just depicted; and yet they manage to possess their souls in patience, and to bear up with manly fortitude and meekness.

But it is not necessary to suppose the worst, and, therefore, not altogether fair or wise, to try your principles by that test. The worst is not a proper test of piety, until God actually apply it by His providence. Let us, therefore, suppose an ordinary medium between the best and the worst.

Take Agur's prayer as your maxim, "Grant me neither poverty nor riches." This is the average lot in your circle. Would, then, this medium please you? It is, upon the whole, the most favorable to piety; but it does not produce piety. You know many who are neither rich nor poor, just as ungodly as the richest or the poorest in the land.

The End

www.ingramcontent.com/pod-product-compliance
Lightning Source LLC
Chambersburg PA
CBHW070118080526
44586CB00013B/1328